philosophy

adventures in thought and reasoning

philosophy

adventures in thought
and reasoning

michael picard

METRO BOOKS
NEW YORK

METRO BOOKS
New York

An Imprint of Sterling Publishing
387 Park Avenue South
New York, NY 10016

This 2012 edition published by Metro Books,
by arrangement with Quid Publishing

Conceived, designed, and produced by
Quid Publishing
Level 4, Sheridan House
114 Western Road
Hove BN3 1DD
England

Design by Tony Seddon

Images on pages 6, 14, 20, 64, 67, 81, 86, 88, 120 © Thinkstock
Images on pages 38, 41, 164 © Corbis
Image on page 44 © Paul D Stewart | Science Photo Library
Images on pages 140, 152 © Getty Images

ISBN: 978-1-4351-4096-7

For information about custom editions, special sales, and premium and corporate purchases,
please contact Sterling Special Sales at 800-805-5489 or specialsales@sterlingpublishing.com.

Manufactured in China

2 4 6 8 10 9 7 5 3 1

www.sterlingpublishing.com

CONTENTS

WHAT IS PHILOSOPHY?

Philosophy, of old the Queen of the Sciences, has come down a notch since her glory days. The rise of modern scientific methods, rather like Cesarean section, has forced the birth of her independent children, the sciences, and one after another they have dropped from her generous womb: first physics, with it physiology, then chemistry, followed later by the social and human sciences, psychology, economics, sociology, etc. Each in its turn abandoned her as they attained to the peerage of departmental status within the academies. Ironically, today she is reputed to be barren, like that ironical old midwife, Socrates himself.

Over the centuries, she has sometimes eked out a living as a handmaiden to the sciences, adding some over-wordy clarification here, performing rhetorical services there, itching rather than scratching out a marginal existence. After withering and puritanical self-criticism, followed by delusions of metaphysical grandeur, more artful and hopeful means of self-destruction were hit upon. Obscure scheming went on covertly to restore the crown of metaphysics to her aging head, with its deeply furrowed brow, but these efforts came to nothing and ended in narcissistic collapse. It is whispered that she spent time in a flophouse for aging beatniks, eating her own heart in existential worry. On last sighting, she had taken the form of an old mare, and was being led into the "desert landscapes" of Quinean ontology, where she is thought to have starved herself on a diet of words.

Scratching Your Head Is Good Exercise

But in spite of her preoccupations, philosophy has not died. Her questions have never been the sole possession of elite minds. The big problems of existence have never gone away, and continue to gnaw at the public viscera. The average person with a house, a job, and a car still wonders what the hell it all means sometimes, and the questions of the have-nots are the same, only that much more urgent. The tomes of the scholars do not reach the wondering masses; their books are all too hard. Yes, there is *Philosophy Now* magazine. But what is needed is a new kind of philosophy book, a book of bite-sized enigmas, manageable mysteries, convenient head-scratchers one can get through in about the time it takes for a bathroom break. What is needed is a book that is not a book. The solution is now in your hands.

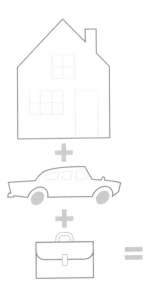

Philosophy Paints Its Grays in Rainbow

This unbook offers an imaginative but very partial tour of the vast terrain of philosophy. The tone is exploratory and non-dogmatic, and throughout the chapters interactive exercises and critical-thinking asides are provided to get you thinking for yourself about the quandaries covered in its pages. An emphasis on the colorful lore of philosophy, as well as a free use of puzzles and narratives, is intended to offset the sometimes technical subject matter.

To begin, a map of the main divisions of philosophy is provided on the next pages. This map, totally contrary to convention, presumes philosophy is on friendly terms with all other disciplines, and accordingly includes them. Far from delimiting a remote and inaccessible region for the specialist philosopher, the net is cast wide, and issues of parallel concern in the various sciences are included, not to resume any imperial presumptions on the part of the dethroned Queen, but only to keep lines of interdisciplinary communication open and to cite landmarks that readers may already know. It is the generous spirit of co-operative tolerance, not any possessive pretensions, that represents philosophy as coextensive with all human knowing.

PHILOSOPHY

Literally, the Love of Wisdom; or the Study of Reality, Knowledge, and Values

Subject	Major Divisions of Philosophy and key subdivisions	Crossover Points (showing points of relatedness despite the major divisions)
Reality Being, God, nature, essence, causation, time, space, self, identity, freedom, infinity, number, necessity, possibility, becoming, function, fact, truth	Metaphysics: A branch of philosophy concerned with anything real, or apparently real. Ontology: The study of being (from *ontos*, the Greek for "being"). Sample issues: Who we really are. What we really are. What there is. What is ultimate? How much do I contribute to my experience of reality? Is order imposed by mind or physical law? By this broad definition, physics is part of metaphysics, distinguished only by its scientific epistemology (its methods). Social science, as the study of social formations, is taken in broadly here.	Unless values or knowledge are real, they are illusions. Necessity makes certainty possible. Purpose and personhood are as much metaphysical as they are ethical concepts. Permission is ethical possibility.

Subject	Major Divisions of Philosophy and key subdivisions	Crossover Points (showing points of relatedness despite the major divisions)
Knowledge Truth, method, doubt, certainty, perception, cognition, errors, bias, paradox, intuition	Epistemology: A branch of philosophy concerned with the conditions and nature of knowledge. Logic: The science of inference; the art of argument. How to reason. Sample issues: What can I know? What should I believe? How can I be sure? Is seeing believing? How is uncertainty to be reduced? By this broad definition, scientific methods are part of epistemology, as is cognitive neuroscience. Sociology of knowledge is another empirical approach to epistemology.	Unless reality or values are known, they are idle theory. Issues of logic within metaphysics: Truth, form, necessity, set, infinity. Moral reasoning involves both logic and ethical values.
Values Right, wrong, good, evil, virtue, purpose, dignity, health, happiness, beauty, the sublime, the holy, money, precaution	Value Theory: A branch of philosophy containing all questions of value; includes, not limited to, aesthetics (theory of art and beauty). Ethics and Morality: Includes, but not limited to, political values (liberty, justice, equality, community) and spiritual values (faith, the sacred, piety, righteousness). Sample issues: What to live for. How to live. What do people want? What is permissible? What is obligatory? What is best? What can I amount to? What may I hope for? By this broad definition, philosophical questions arise also in economics, medicine, politics, and spirituality.	Unless there is value to philosophy, it should not be done. Responsibility is ethical necessity. Truth is a value. Faith is a knowledge claim. Wisdom (what to know) is the pinnacle of epistemology. Freedom is a metaphysical issue, but also a moral, political, and spiritual one.

Epistemology

Epistemology is about the nature and conditions of human knowledge: what is it, and how do we get it? Among its trickiest questions is how reliably to discern genuine knowledge from merely seeming to know, which is far easier and more popular. In this chapter we explore perception, illusions, biases, and doubts, and cast glances at some of the great epistemologists from ancient, early modern, and recent times. A classic definition of knowledge as justified true belief is examined and contested by counter-examples, plus sundry puzzles and problems pertaining to knowledge are briefly presented.

KNOWLEDGE AS
JUSTIFIED TRUE BELIEF

*"At the gates of knowledge the
sceptic stands guard; before we
can enter the citadel we must
answer his challenge."*

—Annas and Barnes (1985)

Knocking (on) Knowledge

Knowledge (what it is, what it requires,
and what it confers) is indisputably
central to the enterprise of philosophy. It
is the subject of that principal branch of
philosophy known as epistemology, a field
that derives its name from the Greek word
for knowledge (*episteme*). But all branches
are intertwined; none of the others could
be the least viable if it were not for
epistemology. It makes no sense to make
claims about what is real or what is
valuable in the absence of claims of
knowledge. Reality and values may be as
they are; if we are without knowledge of
them, all theorizing is vanity. Knowledge is
a gateway into the citadel of philosophy.

And yet some philosophers spend their
entire lives outside those gates, and they
are not all clamoring to get in. Some stand
around belittling the credentials of those
who would enter. These self-appointed
guardians at the gates of knowledge will
ask: *Why? Are you sure? How do you
know? Might it not be otherwise?* Though
annoying, these skeptics have this one
salutary influence: they prevent dogmatism
from entering the ideal city. They prove
something else too: though knowledge be

a way into the fortress of philosophy,
philosophy nevertheless flourishes outside
its own gates. Philosophy exists as a
question, as a *what-if*, before it establishes
an answer, and makes a bid for knowledge.

This chapter on knowledge promises
none. What you will find here is an
assortment of doubts, errors, illusions,
biases, a few doubtful but instructive tales,
a theory or two, even some myths and
legends. Aristotle said that philosophy
begins and has always begun in wonder, and
nothing is so productive of wonder as a little
doubt ... except perhaps a big doubt. There
are some big doubts here, but also a few
knowledge claims. Even those claims you
will have to try out for yourself before you
can be sure, like keys, they open the gates.

EXERCISE

Knowledge is justified true belief, but these
three conditions have also been denied as
unnecessary to knowledge. Can you give
examples of knowledge that is:

>   **not** belief
>   **not** true
> and/or   **not** justified?

Possible answers are shown opposite.

This theory has also been questioned from a
different direction. For instance, counter-
examples have been proposed in which
justified true beliefs do not amount to
knowledge. Try to think of some counter-
examples before reading Gettier (pp. 26–27).

A First Guess at Knowledge

To start, consider a tentative definition already mooted by Plato: *knowledge is justified true belief.* This is intended to work both ways. First, to know something, one must believe it, it must be true, and one must have justification for believing it. Conversely, whatever is believed with justification, and true, is known. The definition is imperfect; you can supply your own critique and challenge your imagination as suggested, but we can begin by looking at its three main parts.

Belief—First, knowledge is a species of belief. Sometimes, when challenged, we say, "I don't *believe* it, I *know!*"—as if knowledge made belief redundant. But belief does not vanish when knowledge arises, unless indeed it is a false belief that knowledge replaces. And then the replacement is a true belief. The point is that you, as an individual, cannot know anything unless you believe it.

Truth—So, to know a proposition, one must believe it. Yet belief alone is insufficient. For starters, the proposition has to be true. But what is truth? In Socratic fashion, we are not asking for examples of truths, but an account of the nature of truth. What does it mean for a proposition to be true in the first place (whether or not it is believed)? This is a metaphysical question, but one of obvious importance to epistemology. We look at it later in this chapter (see pp. 40–43).

Justification—This is about evidence, not excuses. If you believe a truth by accident, it is not knowledge. The way you get to knowledge is part of knowledge. Justification involves giving a rational account, credible reasons to accept or reject a belief, an epistemic warrant.

Experts are authorities; yet it is not their authority, rather their expertise, that should prompt their advice. Expertise must explain itself, it must reason toward its conclusions. Otherwise it is brute authority or fanciful myth.

For Plato, a rational account (a *logos*) was a burden much like this epistemic accountability of experts. Geometric proof and dialectical intuition were his ideals of justification. But Plato also told a lot of fanciful stories, myths he presented as merely probable or similar to truth (such as the myth of Atlantis). And Socrates, introduced next, had his own mysterious means of justification, notably his inner *daemon*, a divine "voice" he obeyed.

Prevailing wisdom, though "common knowledge," may err: there can be false common knowledge.

Knowledge as power, as in sociology of knowledge. Not belief questionably justified.

The study of knowledge claims as social phenomena, usually involving power politics. There is no presumption of truth. Also may exist as cultural practices (rather than as belief).

Organizational knowledge, key in the knowledge economy. Represented not in individual minds but in teams, organizational cultures, increasingly in electronic information systems.

Behavioral learning, based on classical conditioning or history or reinforcement. This assumes Pavlov's dog knows the bell means food.

Acquaintance, and familiarity. These are forms of knowledge hard to reduce to belief, truth, or justification.

Know-how, or procedural knowledge. Knowing how to ride a bike is not just relevant beliefs about bike-riding. It works, but it cannot be said to be true.

Socrates

Socrates was not the first philosopher. Philosophy in Greece was said to have been born when myths died, as a *logos* (rational account) to replace the defunct *mythos* (story or narrative). Thales, by reputation the earliest Greek philosopher, considered the origin of the world to be water. Anaximenes said air. Heraclitus postulated fire as its source and principle, asserting that change alone was constant and that we could never step into the same river twice, for "ever different waters flow" upon us.

The first philosophers were physicalist metaphysicians. Later, learned sophists (literally, "the wise") were drawn to Athens, the democratic center of a rising empire, to proffer advice where it mattered, with the wealthy and powerful. They earned fees by dispensing advice and educating the youth in virtue and/or effectiveness. Oratory and rhetoric, the PR of the day, were indispensable arts in the courts and the political arena. One esteemed sophist was Protagoras, a complex and interesting figure who has been perhaps eclipsed by his most famous line, "man is the measure of all things" (see Moral Relativism, pp. 56–57).

Moral Autonomy as Thinking for Yourself

Socrates was often lumped in with the sophists, but he fit the type poorly. He charged no fees, cared not for money or power, and tried "to follow the argument wherever it leads." Seeking knowledge, rather than effective persuasion, he eschewed rhetorical devices that deceive the audience, trick the mind, and "make the weaker argument look stronger." In other words, Socrates did irony, but he would not spin.

Instead of the sophist tag, Socrates would only lay claim to the more modest term, *philo-sopher* (lover of wisdom). Socrates loved wisdom, but would not pretend to possess it. All he knew, he said, was that he knew nothing. He invited all comers to join him in inquiry. But the search was the discovery. This is just the process of thinking for oneself, of reasoning out moral and epistemological issues, of not taking hand-me-down ideas for granted, nor plausible answers for good enough.

To Socrates, truth and virtue were the same. He held that no one ever does evil intentionally, but only by mistaking what is good or right. By thinking for ourselves, in other words, by striving for moral autonomy, we reduce unintentional evil, and so make our souls as good as possible. But we cannot think for ourselves if we do not come to know ourselves. Self-knowledge is unteachable, but self-knowledge alone is the guarantor of virtue. Thus the fundamental paradox of Socrates: virtue is knowledge, vice is ignorance.

Philosophy as a Mission

A rash young fan of Socrates consulted the ancient Oracle at Delphi, priestess and mouthpiece of Apollo, the god of reason and proportion. He inquired whether there was anyone in Athens wiser than Socrates, to which the god answered no. This puzzled Socrates, since he claimed no wisdom. Avoiding the Confirmation Bias (see p. 17), he devoutly tested the god's assertion, only to find many pretenders to wisdom, but none wise. His search was an education to the noble youth of Athens, but it also meant exposure for epistemic over-reachers, whatever their status or reputation. Socrates made enemies.

In dialogue, Socrates required the individual to have an active conscience in the search for truth. For this, Cornford claimed he "discovered the soul." Taylor, following Burnet, says he "created the conception of the soul" dominant ever since in Western philosophy. Justin Martyr (2nd century BCE) considered Socrates a Christian before Christ, and many other ancient philosophers (Plato, the stoics, the skeptics) claimed Socrates as their forebear. Said Cicero: "All philosophers think of themselves, and want others to think of them, as followers of Socrates."

Despite his professed ignorance, Socrates was knowledgeable in mathematics (see Pythagoras, pp. 88–89) and studied the first Greek philosophers. But he came to regard their metaphysical claims as no better than myths, speculations beyond the reach of human knowledge, beyond even our proper concern. Originally Socrates had high hopes for the philosophy of Anaxagoras, who claimed that the source of the cosmos was not water, air, or fire, but Mind. Socrates felt sure this view was correct, as Mind alone could arrange everything for the best, and ensure each thing served its proper function. But Anaxagoras' book (which no longer exists) disappointed him, for in it Mind apparently only originated the world, after which the usual physical principles arranged things the way we see them now. Socrates' disappointment reveals his implicit teleology: unless the purpose of the world is known, the world is not understood.

The Fate of Socrates

Charged with corrupting youth and atheism, Socrates died by drinking hemlock, under penalty of law. He was the first tragic hero of philosophy.

COGNITIVE BIAS

The Moron and the Maniac

We've all been there. You're late for work and in a hurry, but on the drive you get caught behind a slowpoke idiot who doesn't even know how to get out of the way.

We've all been there. You're driving along sensibly, lawfully, when some maniac storms up behind you, impatient but unable to pass, so they are on your bumper, tailgating. Yet another dangerous jerk. We always find ourselves behind a moron and in front of a maniac. The driver ahead is a moron; we are never the maniac. The driver behind is a jerk; we are never the moron. Our speed is always the correct speed to be going.

Amid the constant chatter of the engaged mind, busy about its daily business, we find our perpetually revised explanations of what is going on around us. We explain peoples' behavior by attributing causes (for example, we blame or make excuses), even if only in the silence of our private thoughts. Psychologists have explored what philosophers have long lamented—our tendency to decide amiss, judge poorly, and misattribute causes. The mind is a biased instrument, and those who use it without taking compensatory precautions are at a constant disadvantage. We must use our flawed tool in order to correct for our flawed tool—a risky proposition.

What Were You Thinking?

As in the above example, we make *personal* attributions to explain the behavior of others (we impugn their motives and scornfully label them), but we make *situational* attributions in our own case (duty beckons, speed limits are in force). Our over-attribution of personal and internal factors in the causes of other peoples' behavior, while downplaying the external demands they are under, is a tendency so pervasive that it has been

---

WASON SELECTION TASK

Imagine that the illustrations below represent cards that have numbers printed on one side and letters on the other. Your job is to confirm whether or not the following rule accurately describes the four cards:

"If there is a vowel on one side, there is an even number on the other."

Which card or cards must you turn over to verify if these cards follow this rule? Answer first, before you check the solution on the opposite page.

WASON SELECTION TASK *correct response*

"If there is a vowel on one side, there is an even number on the other."
You probably guessed the vowel card E. Correct. But did you also check under 7? If there is
a vowel back there, the rule is broken. Unless you check there, you can't confirm the rule.
You may have also guessed 6. Actually, that card is irrelevant to verifying the truth of the rule.
Even if a consonant is there, the rule still stands. Turning over card 6 shows the Confirmation
Bias at work, and also the fallacy of Affirming the Consequent (see Fallacy, pp. 132–133).

Interestingly, people do better with more concrete social situations than with these
abstract stipulated rules. Most people easily solve the following essentially identical
problem correctly. On one side of each card is a person's age, on the other is the beverage
they are drinking.

Confirm this Rule: "If one is drinking beer, one must be over 18."

called the *fundamental attribution* error
and even hailed as the cornerstone of
scientific social psychology.

In explaining our own behavior, we
often demonstrate a *self-serving bias*, as
the example of idiot vs. jerk drivers also
illustrates. When outcomes are positive, we
attribute it to our virtues, our intelligence,
or generally our competence. When
outcomes are negative, we appeal to
circumstance. I passed the test because
I'm so smart. I failed the test, but it was
tricky or unfair. A related fallacy of moral
explanation is age-old: when things go
wrong, we hold others accountable for
outcomes (we point to their incompetence),
but excuse ourselves by good intentions
(I did the best I could!).

Subsequent research has shown that age
and culture influence the incidence of these
errors. Broadly speaking, those from East
Asian cultures commit the fundamental
error less, or not at all. The Japanese show
little self-serving bias. These differences
may be due to a greater rate of situational
attribution in general, or even to more
malleable (more situational) self-identity.
Bicultural individuals may even switch
attribution styles according to context.

EASTERN DOUBT

Ancient Eastern Skepticism

Skepticism is a very ancient philosophy. Whenever uncertainty is the presumption, or doubt is raised to a principle, some form of skepticism is in play. Skepticism is either a philosophical stance within epistemology, or it looks askance at the entire project of coming to know about knowledge. Skepticism can be a very anti-philosophical philosophy. Several of its great historical statements come from outside philosophy proper, from poets, mystics, and religious minds (without whom philosophy would be far poorer than it is). Strangely, believers are often no strangers to doubt.

Ancient Chinese Skepticism

The ancient Taoist philosophy of China distanced itself from all absolute claims to knowledge. Tao (which means "way") is silent and cannot be said or fully conceptualized. The truth that can be known is not the eternal truth. Here are two statements verging on overt skepticism, cautioning all zealous epistemic optimists.

"One who knows, does not speak.
One who speaks does not know."
—Lao Tzu, *Tao Te Ching, Ch. 79*

"Once Chuang Chou dreamed he was a butterfly. He was happy as a butterfly, enjoying himself and going where he wanted. He did not know he was Chou. Suddenly he awoke, whereupon he started to find he was Chou. He didn't know whether Chou had dreamed he was a butterfly, or if a butterfly were dreaming it was Chou. Between Chou and the butterfly, there must be some distinction!"
—Chuang Tzu, *Inner Chapters*

Ancient Indian Uncertainty

"Who knows for certain? Who shall here declare it?
Whence was it born, and whence came this creation?
The gods were born after this world's creation:
Then who can know from whence it has arisen?"
—From *The Hymn of Creation*, in the *Rig-Veda*

There are many myths of creation in Hindu texts, but this one is an honest shrug of the shoulders. Hymns so circumspect drift into philosophy. Note that "the gods" (the innumerable Hindu deities) are born after creation, so they are not to be understood as the world's creator. Rather, they are at most the world's shaper and arranger. This hymn seeks to know what transcends manifest reality, and wisely finishes off with a question mark.

Hinduism is not, in general, a skeptical tradition. In its classic *Vedanta* form, it proclaims not only the laws of karma and reincarnation, but also the existence of a unitary Self, which is the ultimate identity of all things. As this Self (*Atman*) is divine, room for skepticism would seem limited. Yet your realization of our transcendent identity is described as waking up, as if from a dream. Only, this world is the dream you wake from. To say that the physical cosmos is an illusion (*maya*), however, is not to deny its existence. A dream exists: it's just not what it seems to be.

What the Buddha Never Taught

"I have not explained that the world is eternal or that the world is not eternal. I have not explained that the world is finite or that the world is infinite. I have not explained that the soul and body are identical or that the soul and body are not identical. I have not explained that the enlightened sage exists after death or that the enlightened sage does not exist after death. And why have I not explained all this? Because it profits not, nor tends to Supreme wisdom and Nirvana."
—Sutra 63 of *Majjhima-Nikaya*

Siddhartha Gautama the Buddha believed in past lives, and is said to have had a complete vision of all his own. But he dismissed many metaphysical issues as philosophy not conducive to liberation.

Yet the Buddha made a point of doubting the existence of a self or soul. Rebirth can occur without a soul passing from one life to the next, much as one candle causes another to be lit. Rebirth is an effect of the last dying thought, not the continuity of a self through death. Strictly, the Buddhist view is a doctrine of rebirth, not a belief in reincarnation or any "transmigration of souls" as found in Hinduism and Plato. Still, for both Hinduism and Buddhism, death and rebirth can be overcome by enlightenment. This optimism is no skepticism.

Plato

Born of a distinguished Athenian family, Plato was a young man when he fell under the sway of Socrates and became his disciple. After Socrates' death, Plato left Athens for several years before he returned to establish a formal school, the Academy—the forebear of modern universities. His most notable student was Aristotle (see pp. 64–65 and 90–91).

The trial and death of Socrates must have deeply wounded Plato, and he later wrote vivid accounts of the events. Much of what we know of Socrates comes to us from Plato. Plato's own philosophy emerged gradually, and can in some ways be understood as his vindication of the life and mission of Socrates. Plato's world had failed him, and the ideals Socrates pointed to were nowhere to be found in the Athenian

democratic system or in the conduct of the powerful. Socrates had shown integrity was possible, but its sources were inward, not in the prevailing wisdom or the existing social order.

Socrates had resisted mischief and seemed incorruptible, regardless of the inducements. He even refused to escape from prison and his sentence when escape was made possible. What invisible knowledge did he possess that enabled him to overcome all baser motives and rise above the politics of wealth and power? What must Socrates have known to render him virtuous even in the face of death? Perhaps the world is not what it appears to be.

More than Meets the Eye

The question of knowledge became vital to Plato, but the visible world with its injustice and corruption could not be the source of it. The eyes give us color and light, but more than the senses is needed to recognize objects (as in simple observational judgments like, "This is a book"). Even for that we require mind, an inner intelligence (*nous*). In one dialogue, Plato has Socrates, solely by asking questions, lead a boy uneducated in mathematics to prove to himself a certain geometrical theorem. No one ever told the boy the theorem; Socrates only put questions to him. *How did the knowledge get into the boy if nobody else put it there?* You can try this for yourself as an exercise in Socratic dialogue, Digging for Inner Diamonds, on pp. 22–23.

Spelunking with Plato

Plato's theory of knowledge and his metaphysical views are represented in his famous *Allegory of the Cave*.

According to this, our life is like those of prisoners chained in a cave, who only see shadows cast on a wall from a fire behind them. If we are freed and led out of the cave, we see the objects themselves, like those that cast the shadows. We see the originals, whereas earlier we had known only copies.

Gradually, we learn to see the heavenly bodies, and learn mathematics and the music of the spheres. This gives us insight into the eternal truths beyond the physical world.

This celebrated allegory encapsulates in story form the technical aspects of Plato's epistemology and his metaphysics. He represents them on a divided line.

Metaphysically, Plato divides reality into two. On the one hand there is the physical world (which, as Heraclitus said, is in constant flux) given to us by the senses. On the other, there is a constant, ideal realm intelligible only to the intellect ("Plato's Heaven").

For Plato, the social and natural world (the only reality most people ever know) is but an illusion, and like a dream. Above our physical heaven another realm exists where the ideal forms of Justice, Truth, and Beauty dwell—a place where our minds may also go, and where they may know a kinship and belonging.

The philosopher breaks free of the chains of social convention and popular taste, and ascends outside the cave of our world.

The Duty to Descend: Stooping to Rule

However akin the mind (or highest function of the soul) may be to the ideal forms that dwell in that higher reality, the freed philosopher is nevertheless bound by an obligation to return to the social world and to work here to implement this vision of the good. In the end, philosophers have a duty of service to offer the world. Like Socrates, the true philosopher will not remain isolated in lofty meditation outside the cave, but will carry those values back into the world. This represents the leadership responsibility born of wisdom.

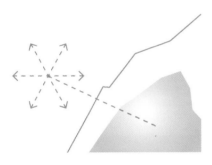

Grades of Being (metaphysics)	Invisible, immutable, eternal, ideal		Visible, changing, ephemeral, real	
	Ethical forms (the Good)	Mathematical forms	Physical objects	Fleeting shadows
Grades of Knowing (epistemology)	Intelligence = intuitive reason	Thinking = understanding	Belief = faith, conviction	Imagining = appearing
	Dialectical	Deductive	True opinion	Everyday reality
	KNOWLEDGE		**OPINION**	

1 Digging for Inner Diamonds

THE PROBLEM:

Draw a small square on a blank, unlined sheet of paper, somewhere near the center of the page. Suppose that the length of each side is one unit. Your task is simply to construct a new square with twice the area of the original square.

THE METHOD:

Socrates reportedly posed this problem to an uneducated slave boy, and was able to lead the boy to success merely by asking questions. That is, Socrates gave the boy no new information and no instruction in geometry. Yet the lad, prodded by the right questions, was able to obtain a correct answer, and to construct a square with twice the area of the original. Can you?

Here are some questions to help you along. Now most readers will have some level of background in high-school geometry, and thus have some advantage over the ancient youth, who before that day was innocent of all mathematics. The boy's accomplishment led Plato to a remarkable conclusion, and your own, if you are successful, might provide some small additional confirmation. As you work through your response, guided by the following Socratic questions, ask yourself what Plato's remarkable conclusion might have been.

1. We had agreed to call the length of one side of the original square one unit. So to start we can ask an easy question: What is the area of the original square? What is the formula for determining the area of a square from the length of its sides? How many "square units" are in the original square?

2. Once you have the number of square units in the original square, recall that we need a square that encloses twice that area. This should allow you easily to answer the second question: What is the area of the sought-after square? How many square units need to be in the square to be constructed?

3. The next question is obvious, but harder to answer: How long do the sides of the new square need to be if its area is twice that of the original square? That is, since you now know the required area, and you know the desired figure is a square, how long do its sides have to be? (It may help here

to recall your answer to the general question raised above: what is the relation of the length of the sides of a square to its area?)

4. If you have successfully answered the above questions, you know how long the sides of the needed square are required to be. Now you only need to obtain a line of that length, use that line as one of your sides, and the desired square will be constructed. But where will you find a line of the needed length?

5. Go back to the original square. Draw a diagonal line from one corner to another. Ask yourself: how long is that diagonal line (called the hypotenuse)? What is the area of a square built upon that diagonal (like a diamond)?

6. The answer to that last question may be obvious. If it is not, here are a few final leading hints: the area of the square of the hypotenuse is equal to the sum of what two squares? (If even this is no help to you, you can ruin your innocence entirely by flipping to pp. 88–89 on Pythagoras.)

THE SOLUTION:

By a series of Socratic questions, but no new information, you (or perhaps only the slave boy of old) have been led to a new truth. The boy at least had no prior knowledge of geometry, no previous instruction in mathematics; yet through appropriate questioning he was shown to have all he needed within himself to obtain a correct answer. Since he did not obtain this knowledge from Socrates or during his lifetime, Socrates concluded the boy must have known it at birth, from non-sensory experiences prior to birth. In short, this story is part of the Socratic argument for the existence of innate knowledge (see pp. 28–29, 38). The knowledge of mathematics, Socrates reasoned, was already within each of us, even if we have to struggle so hard to get to an answer.

Education on this Socratic view consists in "drawing out" truths already installed in the soul. Thus Socrates' so-called nativism does not mean that the innate knowledge we all carry within us will reveal itself easily and without struggle. Instead, that process may be as difficult and painful as pulling teeth or proving theorems. And there are those amongst us who fear knowledge as much as they fear the dentist.

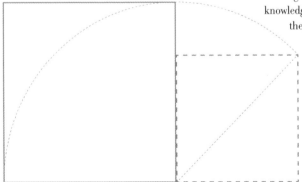

WESTERN DOUBT

Doubt has been a friend to philosophy from its earliest days. The first great Western skeptics are surrounded in legend, even while they attack legend. And they attack knowledge, too, even its very possibility. While this seems like a counsel of epistemic despair, it keeps the critical spirit alive. Skepticism has died many times, but whenever it has been reborn, the spirit of philosophy has been revived.

Xenophanes

Xenophanes, a poet-philosopher from around the 6th century BCE, exists only as reports and in literary fragments. He was a believer ("God is one, supreme among gods and men") but stopped short of claiming full certainty ("These things have seemed to me to resemble the truth"). He also adopted a highly skeptical stance toward the stories told by esteemed poets like Homer and Hesiod, especially when they represented the gods with human foibles (like jealousy, wrath, and sexual indiscretion). He scorned popular credulity.

"Mortals suppose that the gods are born (as they themselves are) and that they wear man's clothing and have human voice and body. But if cattle or lions had hands so as to paint ... and produce works of art as men do, they would paint their gods and give them bodies in form like their own—horses like horses, cattle like cattle."
—T. V. Smith (ed.) 1956, p. 14

Pyrrho of Elis

Pyrrho is the earliest known extreme Greek skeptic (ca. 360–217 BCE). Legend has it that epistemic nihilism was his response to witnessing a self-incendiary sage from India, one of the "naked sages" or yogis who accompanied Alexander the Great on his military retreat from India. He was present when Kalanos, an Indian holy man who had apparently become ill on the trip and was ready to die, requested a pyre be built, atop which he climbed. At his signal, he and it went up in flames. The tranquillity and self-control (*ataraxia*) that went into this self-immolation impressed Pyrrho. Such imperturbability (in contrast, for example, to possession of truth) came increasingly to characterize the ideal philosopher, impervious to pain, complete in self-mastery, but absent all belief.

A similarly extreme skeptical stance, formulated more as a riposte or a rhetorical flourish than as a position to be defended, is expressed by the Sophist Gorgias, in his devastating three-point unphilosophy:

1. Nothing exists.
2. If it did, we couldn't know it.
3. If we knew it, we couldn't communicate it.

The very criterion of truth, by which we distinguish truth and falsity, must pass its own test. For if it doesn't, it is a false criterion. But if it does, the argument will be logically circular: the criterion is true because it is true. A criterion of truth can no more be self-validating than a judge can serve justice as judge of his own case. So no criterion of truth can be shown to be true.

DESCARTES' METHOD OF DOUBT

Skepticism of various forms thrived in ancient times as critical inquiry and polemical critique. Like much ancient learning, it eventually died out and was forgotten in Europe. When it was reintroduced in the 16th century, it added fuel to the fire of conflict in matters of spiritual authority and scientific inquiry. Descartes' so-called "method of doubt" was actually aimed at establishing certainties, and thus at refuting absolute skepticism, and the pyrrhonism then undergoing a resurgence.

Descartes was no skeptic. He used skeptical methods only to arrive at indubitable truth. He tried to doubt everything, even to imagine that the obvious were false. But his "general demolition of opinion" was not total, for he uncovered an orderly set of propositions he could recommend by their absolute certainty. It was impossible to doubt them.

Descartes noted that the senses sometimes deceive us (see Optical Illusions, pp. 30–31). He observed that trusted teachers and great philosophers occasionally turned out to be wrong. The physical world as it is given to us seems real enough, but dreams can seem equally real while they last. Simple counting verifies the addition of small sums (like 2+3), but it is just possible that an all-powerful evil genius could routinely insert a false answer into our mind at the proper moment: we only *think* the true sum is 5.

Doubting all this, Descartes experienced vertigo, but he righted himself by finding a fixed point on which to anchor all the rest. He found an unshakable truth no doubt could assail. *He existed*, since it was he who doubted. Let the evil demon do his worst—if Descartes was deceived, he was really deceived, so he had to be real. My experience proves that I exist. The existence of the self (which Descartes also called mind, spirit, or soul) became his starting point, his first fixed principle, invulnerable—*he thought*—to any assault by skeptics.

GETTIER PROBLEMS

What, then, is knowledge? What are its qualities? For more than 2000 years, philosophers broadly accepted the view put forward by Plato that knowledge—in the sense of certainty about propositions—is "justified true belief." To know something is to believe, with good reason, that it is true.

Then, in the 1960s, Edmund Gettier suggested there could be situations in which justified true belief might not constitute knowledge. The scenarios that he used as examples have become known as the Gettier Problems, and the best known of these concerns Messrs Smith and Jones, who are contenders for the same job.

PROBLEM 1:

Having heard the news from a reliable source, Smith believes that Jones has got the job. He also knows that Jones has ten coins in his pocket. Smith validly infers that the job is going to a man with ten coins in his pocket.

Unknown to Smith, however, he himself got the job. Just by coincidence, he happens to have ten coins in his own pocket, though he doesn't know it. So Smith's conclusion is right: the job did go to a man with ten coins in his pocket. His inference was valid, the conclusion is true, and his source was authoritative, if in error. Yet, despite his belief being justified and true, can we really call this knowledge?

PROBLEM 2:

In another of his counter-examples, Gettier puts forward a situation in which Smith has the justified belief that Jones owns a Ford. In the proposition "Either P or Q," if P is true then Q can be anything at all and the proposition will still be true, so, confident that Jones owns a Ford, Smith justifiably concludes that "Jones owns a Ford, or Brown is in Barcelona," even though he has no knowledge of where Brown actually is.

In fact, Jones owns a Chevy, but Brown does happen to be in Barcelona, so Smith had a belief that was both true and justified, but was not—says Gettier—knowledge.

SOLUTIONS:

One solution to the problem is to say that it's not a problem—that justified true belief (JTB) is a fine definition of knowledge and that Smith did have knowledge. On the other hand, if you think that the Gettier cases reveal an inadequacy in the classic definition, what could be changed or added to improve it as an account of knowledge? Several philosophers have suggested various fourth conditions that must also be met.

No False Premises

In each of the two problems outlined above, Smith's JTB is founded on a false premise—a JFB, if you like. Jones hadn't been given the job, and Jones didn't own a Ford, but in each case Smith had derived a true justified belief from his false justified belief. One way to avoid the problems posed by these examples would be to say a JTB derived from a false premise does not constitute knowledge. However, it is possible to provide problematic examples in which there do not seem to be false premises. If you believe that someone is in a room because you think you have seen them, when in fact you saw a lifelike dummy, there is no inference from a premise at all—simply a judgment based on visual observation. So, if the person is actually in the room, although you haven't seen them, does your justified true belief constitute knowledge?

A Causal Link

Another approach, put forward by Alvin Goldman, is to require that there should be an "appropriate" causal relationship between the truth of the matter and the subject's belief. For the JTB to count as knowledge, the truth must give rise to the belief and the belief holder should be able to reconstruct the causal chain between the two. On this basis, the lack of this condition in the examples above accounts for the JTB not being knowledge. There does remain, however, the small matter of defining what makes a causal chain "appropriate" or in some way reliable.

Indefeasible Belief

In the late 1960s, Keith Lehrer and Thomas Paxson proposed that a JTB only constitutes knowledge if there is no other piece of information that, if the subject were aware of it, would void or annul the belief. A belief is indefeasible if no other information would override it. In the first example, if Smith had been aware that Jones was not in fact being given the job, it would have overridden and voided his belief that the job was going to a man with ten coins in his pocket. His JTB is not, therefore, knowledge, say Paxson and Lehrer. Unfortunately, placing this requirement upon knowledge might result in a lot of babies being thrown out with the bathwater.

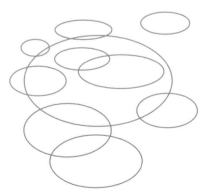

WHAT WERE YOU BORN KNOWING?

Innate vs. Acquired Knowledge

Innate literally means "inborn." If knowledge is justified true belief, innate human knowledge should surely be zero. What belief does a mind have prior to experience? What evidence does the newborn possess prior to first consciousness? If it is not born ready for its experience, how else will it acquire knowledge? But can readiness be knowledge?

What is innate is a readiness or potential for experience and for the acquisition of knowledge. But how are we to characterize a readiness, a mere potentiality, or a so-called disposition? Readiness has to be specific: to be ready for everything is to be ready for nothing.

But not too specific: the human newborn is not ready to acquire English *per se*, but any human language.

Experiments have shown that newborns can remember songs played while they were still in the womb. The infants show a preference, relative to music not played earlier, by a more vigorous sucking on a nipple rigged to register the force. Can infants, then, be born knowing songs? Certainly, familiarity—even if it is a basis for knowledge—is not justified true belief. What is learning for the psychologist is not knowledge for the philosopher (certainly not for the philosopher who sticks to that "platonic" definition of knowledge).

The newborn's eyes will blink at a puff of air; its hand will grasp an adult fingertip that touches its tiny palm; its head will turn toward a brush of its cheek, rooting for the nipple. But these fixed action patterns are all behavioral.

Behaviors may be know-how, but are they knowledge? Are they true or false? Can action be the basis of knowledge?

Innate Mechanisms: INSTINCTS VS. DRIVES

Instincts are unlearned, characteristic patterns of response controlled by specific triggering stimuli in the world. Examples are nesting in birds, which is untaught, and a variety of animal hunting and mating behavior. By itself instinct is inadequate as explanation for human action.

Drives are psychological states arising in response to a physiological need, like hunger, thirst, or sex. They demand to be satisfied, but behavior to do so is not specified, and far more flexible. In the case of sex, some people can live fulfilled lives without it.

Empiricism: All knowledge derives from the senses and sensory experience.

Nativism: We are born with predispositions that enable knowledge or complex behavior to arise in response to experience.

Rationalism: Reason is productive of truth apart from the senses.

Philosophers have been divided on the importance of innate knowledge. Some have denied we have any, insisting that, prior to experience, the newborn's mind is empty, like a blank slate (Aristotle), or a blank page (Locke), waiting for experience to write characters upon it. Such views are called *empiricist* (after a Greek word meaning "experience"). On this view, the senses are the primary, if not sole, fount of knowledge. Hobbes and Hume are other classic empiricist philosophers.

After Darwin, empiricism increasingly recognized a major role for heredity and inborn tendencies. But this was a nativism of instinct, of feeling, of action. The newly born child-mind was still understood as a blank slate, without ideas before experience comes along to furnish them.

However, even if the fetus on the brink of birth has no beliefs, ideas, or knowledge, empiricist philosophers have often allowed and even insisted that we are born with certain innate dispositions to know, with specific potentials for experience (for example, color vision), with readiness for definite epistemic achievements (such as the acquisition of our mother tongue). Empiricists who embrace innate dispositions to know may become indistinguishable from their erstwhile opponents, the *rationalists*, who belabor the importance of innate knowledge and also, more broadly, all the truths reason can discover independent of the senses (see *a priori* knowledge, p. 44). Rationalists are often quite content to claim that the knowledge said to be innate is only potentially there.

Descartes, for instance, is famous for his insistence on innate ideas. But he makes clear that they are specific tendencies, not preformed contents awaiting first witness. He even compares innate ideas to gout, a crippling inflammatory disease that runs in families. The child does not have the illness at birth, but only a hereditary predisposition to develop it. Leibniz, another great rationalist, uses a more poetic image: Innate ideas are like veins in a sculptor's marble block, which predispose the stone to yield one statuary figure rather than another.

Noam Chomsky (see pp. 38–39) revived rationalism in the 20th century with his theories of universal grammar, and of an innate mechanism in an initial state at birth, but capable of being programmed in effect through experience to acquire the knowledge of grammar. Experience, he says, is simply not enough to yield complex grammatical knowledge without presupposing a biologically endowed language acquisition device in a newborn's brain. The scientific problem is to characterize it correctly.

OPTICAL ILLUSIONS

Where Is the Bent Pencil?

A pencil in a glass of water appears to be broken or jagged. The senses can be deceiving. But we can also satisfy ourselves that the pencil, despite appearances, is straight. For one thing, we can feel it with our fingers. If vision is deceiving, it is correctible by another sense, the sense of touch.

But there is a deeper point here. Granted there is an illusion and that the pencil is in reality straight, but your visual experience of jaggedness must itself be something, even while it fails to match reality. The very fact of the pencil's deviation proves that it exists, at least as a mental representation.

The bent pencil exists in mental or phenomenal space, much as dreams are quite real as phenomena—only they are not what they seem. The bent pencil you immediately see is a mental representation of the reality; you never really see reality directly.

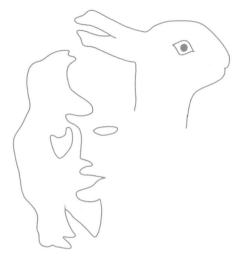

The Quacking Rabbit and the Saxy Lady

The image above can be perceived as a woman's face. Alternatively, there is a cartoon silhouette of a large-nosed, big-eared man playing a saxophone.

Can you see the woman and the man at the same time?

Now look at the topmost image—is it a duck facing left or a rabbit facing right? Can you see the image as a duck and a rabbit at the same time? Most people report difficulty fusing the two perceptions at once, although with practice an amalgam can be achieved.

The same sensory stimulation can result in not one but two perceptions. Sensation is not perception. Perception goes beyond sensory information, by providing an interpretation of it.

Mental representation, then, including sensory perception, involves a sensory and a cognitive component. Subjective reality is both sensory and interpretive.

Subjective Surfaces: An Unconscious Inference?

In the image below, the translucent rectangular surface that appears to hover over the spots does not exist. It is called a *subjective surface*, which is to say it exists only in your mind. The sensory stimulus consists of a number of light circles with carefully arranged darker portions of them.

The great physicist and physiologist Hermann von Helmholtz claimed that the existence of the subjective surface, which is not given in the physical stimulus, results from an unconscious inference, a cognitive act of which we are not even aware. This applies not only to optical illusions, to seeing depth in two-dimensional drawing, and indeed to perception as a whole. Perception is more than mere sensation; it is sensation plus inference. Unconscious inferences, Helmholtz tells us, are normally irresistible, inductive in character, and based on analogies formed through experience.

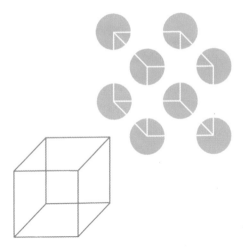

Inverting What Isn't There

The upper of the two images above is subject to five interpretations, and supports five distinct perceptions.

The simplest but perhaps least obvious is eight divided dark circles. But one can also see a cube made of light bars. The cube may seem to stand out above a spotted background; the bars then seem to complete themselves, filling in their implied portions. Even more remarkable, that cube, which but for your mind would not quite exist, can also be reversed. It is a reversible Necker cube, like the one shown above left, which spontaneously inverts, appearing alternately to stick out of the page and jut back into the page. (Watch the spots appear to change spatial location during inversion.) It is impossible to see both cubes at once.

The subjective Necker cube above right can be interpreted in yet other ways. Imagine that the dark circles are holes in a gray wall, through which you can see a cube. This partially hidden cube can also be inverted.

PERCEPTION

A powerful idea running through philosophy and psychology regarding perception is that we are only ever immediately aware of the contents of our own mind. Awareness and knowledge of the world outside us is indirect, mediated by our mental representation. In the first instance, your perceptions are your world. Nothing comes closer to you, and you cannot go around your representation and grasp external reality as it is in itself.

Take a Paradoxical Plunge

Try this experiment at home. Take three buckets of water, one cold, one room temperature, and one hot. Arrange them in order in front of you, and now plunge your hands into the water; for instance, the right hand in the cold water and the left hand in the hot water. Wait half a minute, then take both your hands out and immerse them in the bucket with room-temperature water. How warm does that water now feel?

With the cold right hand you should feel the water to be warm. With the hot left hand you should feel the water to be cold. So which is it? Is the water warm or cold?

This child-safe puzzle, due to the illustrious John Locke (1632–1704), is comparable to the famous old puzzle about the tree that falls in the forest when there is no one around to hear it. Does the tree make a sound? The resolution in both cases consists of a distinction that is as plausible as it is astounding in its implications.

Subjective vs. Objective

Words for perceptual qualities, like *sound*, *hot*, *cold*, are ambiguous. If by sound one means oscillations in local air pressure, then no doubt sounds do radiate as waves from the falling tree, even if no ear and no one is there to perceive it. But if by *sound* one means the immediate object of auditory experience, then clearly no such subjective sound exists. The physical sound is there even without a witness; but there is nothing heard without a hearer. There is no subjective sound without a subject.

It is one thing to know what a high note sounds like, quite another to know that high notes are associated with rapid oscillations in air pressure. There were musicians before there were physicists.

The subjective experience of high or low may be caused by fast or slow oscillations, but subjective reality (that sweet sound) is not identical with the measurable reality. Experience is yet inexplicable in physical terms.

Kicking Around Ideas

Irish philosopher and bishop, George Berkeley (1685–1753) denied the reality of matter, or indeed anything outside a mind. His famous principle was *To be is to be perceived* (he also held the converse): existence was mere occurrence to a mind, being the object of a mind. He considered Newtonian gravitation an occult force (it was, after all, action at a distance). How can the earth attract the moon or even so much as an apple *without even touching them?*

Famous lexicographer and wit, Samuel Johnson (1709–84) is said to have kicked a stone to disprove Berkeley's immaterialism: "I refute it thus!" Of course, Berkeley never said one could not kick a stone. Presumably, however, the foot idea, the stone idea, and the idea of kicking would all have to exist in the same mind.

Explicable and Inexplicable Differences

Heat is likewise ambiguous. If by *heat* one means the mean kinetic energy (average molecular speed), then heat exists whether or not it is felt. The average velocity of the water molecules in the middle bucket, though altered by the introduction of our hands, is not different for each hand. If by *heat* one means the experience of intense warmth, it differs in each hand, but the physical reason for this is quite explicable. In fact, the nerves involved are not registering the temperature of the water at all, but only the change in temperature of the hands. This change moves in a different direction in each hand, though both move toward the temperature of the water in the middle bucket.

Vision suffers a deeper duality. Colors are not intersubjectively comparable. You and I may readily agree that these bananas and those cut pineapples are yellow, but we cannot determine if our experiences of yellow are similar. You'll never know what yellow looks like to me. Could physiology ever overcome this incommensurability?

As Plain as the Nose In Front of Your Face

English philosopher G. E. Moore (1873–1958) attempted to prove *the reality of the world external to the mind* by asserting, flat-footedly, as he held up one hand, "This is a hand!" It was a common-sense revolution in philosophy.

Are you convinced by Moore's simple proof? If yes, what would it take to make you doubt it, even a little? If not, what kind of evidence would persuade you?

PROBLEMS OF SELF-REFERENCE

There Are Two Errors in the the Sentence Shown Here

So what are the two errors? You may have spotted the first one, although most people do not. The sentence contains a duplicate of one word, but since the two instances are on separate lines our brains tend to gloss over this mistake. But what is the second one? Well, there doesn't appear to be one. There is only one error, so the sentence is wrong. But if the sentence is wrong in stating that there are two errors when there is only one, then there is a second error in the sentence. In that case, the sentence is correct, so there isn't a second error, in which case the sentence is mistaken in stating that there is a second error in the sentence, in which case … you get the point.

In the example above, the root of the paradox lies in the fact that the statement refers to itself. In the same way, statements such as "I always lie" sow the seeds of their own impossibility. If this statement is true, then it must also be false!

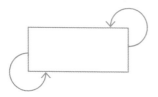 

QUESTION AND ANSWER

Which Is the Right Door?

Let us suppose that you are walking through a labyrinth and you come to a fork in the passageway, each path closed off by a door. One will lead you to your goal, while the other is the doorway to certain death. Each door is guarded by a sentinel who knows what lies beyond, and you are allowed to ask one question in order to open the correct door and reach your goal. However, one of the sentinels always lies and the other one always tells the truth, and you don't know which is which. What question will you ask?

The Solution

What question should you ask the liar or the truth-teller? The question—asked of either of them—that will result in the right answer is, "If I were to ask the other sentinel, which door will lead me to my goal, what would his answer be?" By asking a question that involves both sentinels' answers, you know that the answer will always be false. The truth-teller will tell you the truth about the other sentinel's lie, and the liar will tell you a lie about the other sentinel's truth. Either way, the answer is false. Take the other door!

Eye and Brain

If you've ever assumed that when you read you are looking at all the letters in order to understand each word, try this.

Aoccdrnig to rscheearch by a Biritsh uinervtisy, it deosn't mttaer in waht oredr the ltteers in a wrod are. The olny iprmoatnt tihng is taht the frist and lsat ltteers are in the rghit pclae. The rset can be a toatl mses and you can sitll raed it wouthit a porbelm. Tihs is bcuseae we do not raed ervey lteter by itslef but the wrod as a wlohe.

In fact, the statement is not entirely true. The rest can't actually be a total mess, because certain rearrangements make words more difficult to comprehend than others. The paragraph above also uses generally short or familiar words, and the three-letter words remain unaltered, of course, enabling you to keep track of the structure of the sentences. In general, the rearrangement consists of swapping adjacent letters, and this also helps. You may have had no problem with porbelm, but you would have found pborelm harder. It is also more difficult to identify a word if the rearrangement makes a proper word itself (for example, slate and stale). So there's more to the trick than just keeping the first and last letters in their places. Have a look at these examples, which you will probably find progressively more difficult.

An upexenldod Snoced Wrold War bmob was selscufuscly desfued odutsie the haduqertares of the Alticrugure Mistriny in Pairs yeastdery anterfoon.

Big tax ineesacrs tihs yaer hvae seezueqd the inmcoes of mnay pneosenirs.

A dootcr has aimttded the magltheuansr of a tageene ceacnr pintaet who deid aetfr a hatospil durg blendur.

Words in which letter groupings that produce a single sound have been broken up are particularly hard—take magltheuansr (manslaughter), for example. Incidentally, no British university appears to take credit for this discovery, according to Matt Davis of Cambridge University, who has done considerable research into the secubjt.

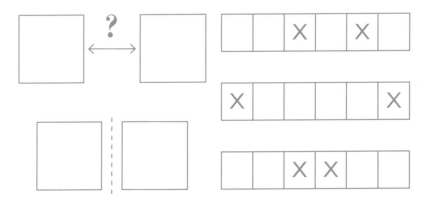

THE PROBLEM:

Take two empty toilet paper rolls, and attach distinct images to one end of each tube, facing inward where vertical and horizontal stripes are used for images. (To start, use identical stripes of different orientation. Later, try pairs of divergent images, such as a male and a female face.) Now bring the tubes together and up to your eyes, as if they were binoculars, taking care to point your eyes and the tubes toward a window or a brightly and evenly lit white wall. Each eye is receiving a distinct image: one of horizontal and one of vertical stripes. Now watch and wait. What happens? How does it change over time?

THE METHOD:

Do not strain to look. Relax the muscles around the eyes as you observe. Passively observe what occurs to see if something stable emerges. How long does it last? What happens when it ends? Try the experiment a few times, allowing plenty of time on each trial for successive changes to take place, and record what you see.

At first you see or can see either image, then you may notice a kaleidoscopic jumble of images; an unstable, jagged edge between the images may form and fail. What is going on here? Can you describe the visual effect?

Later one image may come to dominate, while the other image disappears entirely from view, even though the eye looking at it is still open and operative. What happens to the disappeared image? How does the mind fail to see what its own eye is looking directly at? Have you temporarily gone blind in a fully functional eye?

Remarkable enough, but don't stop yet. Keep the eyes relaxed and stay watching. What changes? If you wait patiently, examining the dominant image, something even stranger will occur. The once recessive and unseen image mounts a return, and the first image fades out of awareness. The stimulation to both eyes remains the same throughout. Why does the system switch from one to another and then, if you wait yet longer, back again? Why do the images begin to oscillate, each taking turns basking in the focus of attention, while the other languishes in an unconscious limbo?

THE SOLUTION:

The phenomenon you are experiencing is called *binocular rivalry*. The two eyes normally work together, having similar but slightly different perspectives on a scene, due to being a few inches apart in the skull. The visual system extracts useful information from the similarities and from the differences in retinal images, and also from the systematically related changes in them as we, with our eyes, move about through space. Whenever we are open-eyed, there are distinct images on the retinas at the back of each of our eyeballs; yet altogether we see one world, not two. (You can get a sense of the two images by opening and closing each eye in turn as you gaze at a distant wall with one finger raised a short distance in front of your face.)

In the present experiment, however, the images cannot be fused. The initial kaleidoscopic jumble that you see arises from your brain's attempt to fuse the unfuseable. When that fails, the brain pursues its perpetual search for sense by settling on one image, and inhibiting the other. The inhibited image is chased out of consciousness, although it remains on the retina and continues to be processed in the brain's primary visual cortex—a point that has been shown by neuro-imaging. As part of an effort to locate (visual) consciousness in the brain, scientists have found an area deeper inside the brain whose activity correlates with the reported stable appearance of one image.

One theory is that certain brain areas processing the recessive image are inhibited (that is, their electrical activity is reduced) by areas processing the dominant image. Inhibitory activity fatigues the cells, thus gradually weakening their supremacy, allowing the recessive image to emerge again into consciousness. The cells responsible for the now-dominant image inhibit their neighbors, but inhibitory activity is exhausting, so this pride of place also fades, and the cycle begins again. This theory is far from the whole story, however, since properties of the suppressed stimulus (such as salience, contrast, and change) influence the duration of the suppression yet more strongly (Uttal, 1981).

A similar rivalry goes on at a conceptual level in such optical illusions as the duck–rabbit (see pp. 30–31). We can't perceive the figure as *both* a duck and a rabbit at the same time, so the interpretation oscillates and switches. This is perhaps the result of a representational rivalry, similar to binocular rivalry. Duck representations inhibit rabbit representations, and vice versa. The brain itself may yet be the venue of a general competition among neural representations at every level. Only those representations that prevail, however fleetingly, poke their heads into the stream of our consciousness, before sinking again into the unconscious oblivion within, teeming with failed suitors for our miserly attention.

Noam Chomsky

theorem. The questions did not contain sufficient information to prove the theorem, so the boy must have contributed knowledge he already possessed without knowing it. This knowledge was drawn out of him, not inserted into him by instruction. Plato concluded that the boy must have had it in him all along, and acquired it in a previous existence.

> **"Plato's problem, then, is to explain how we know so much, given that the evidence available to us is so sparse."**
> —Chomsky, 1986

During language acquisition, Chomsky argued, the child is not tutored in grammar, but is led—by mere interaction—to manifest grammatical knowledge of a particular language. Children come to know the grammar of their native tongue—not, indeed, in the way a language teacher does who is able to explain it, but as demonstrated in practice by their following rules in the production and interpretation of sentences in that language. For Chomsky, the experiential input the child has (the set of all the sentences it has ever heard) is—like Socrates' questions—impoverished; that is, insufficient to account for the knowledge of grammar that the child can actually demonstrate. Having heard only finitely many sentences, it is able to recognize infinitely many potential sentences as grammatical or not. The stimulus of social interaction cannot account for the linguistic competence that emerges. A child who acquires English did not have English grammar in her all along; but she must have had some innate capacity or predisposition that, together with the impoverished experiential input, yielded this remarkable infinitistic competence.

Chomsky is a major political voice as well as a leading theoretical linguist, whose attempts to understand human knowledge of language have transformed the philosophy of mind and language, and stimulated allegiance and dissent in many areas of empirical psychology. A philosophical rationalist, he places himself in a tradition stretching back through Descartes to Plato. He sees the "cognitive revolution" he helped to foment over the last five decades as a resurgence of early modern rationalism. The innate knowledge Chomsky postulated tackled the unique human capacity to acquire a language.

Plato's Problem: Poverty of the Stimulus

Chomsky compared the problem a child faces in acquiring a language to the problem faced by the slave boy in Plato's *Meno*. Untutored in geometry, the boy is yet led—by mere questions—to prove a particular geometrical

The Theory of Grammar as a Theory of Mind

Chomsky even agrees that only this innate capacity (which he called *universal grammar*) was acquired through previous existence. But rather than the pre-existence of the soul or reincarnation, Chomsky appealed to human evolutionary history. Biology has endowed the newborn infant's brain with a specialized device for acquiring any human language, given appropriate inputs. At this level, the study of the human capacity for language is a study of genetic endowment.

"Universal grammar ... may be regarded as a characterization of the genetically determined language faculty. One may think of this faculty as a 'language acquisition device,' an innate component of the human mind that yields a particular language through interaction with presented experience, a device that converts experience into a system of knowledge attained: knowledge of one or another language."
—Chomsky, 1986

Chomsky thought of the language acquisition device as a language organ in the brain. We grow a language, rather than learn it. He came to conceive of this device as a biological machine with a finite number of switches set by early language experience. Set in one way, the machine would know English grammar; set another way, Swahili or Japanese. All possible human languages would be represented in the various settings of these switches.

Beyond Surface Word Order: The Invisibility of Grammar

Word order is important to meaning. It makes a difference whether dog bites man or man bites dog. But surface word order is not sufficient to determine meaning. The words must also be assigned grammatical roles, and this can sometimes be done in different ways for the exact same word order.

To illustrate this, consider first these similar-sounding sentences:

1. Time flies like an arrow.

2. Fruit flies like a banana.

Flies is a verb in 1, but a noun in 2. *Like* is a preposition in 1, a verb in 2. But these are only the most natural readings of 1 and 2. Each can be interpreted in both ways.

The following sentences are also grammatically ambiguous. They are *amphibolies*, each having two meanings. Distinguish these meanings and identify the different grammatical roles played by individual words (as below):

Flying planes can be dangerous.

The lamb is too hot to eat.

The shooting of the hunters was terrible.

They are cooking apples.

Visiting relatives can be a nuisance.

There are three stock theories of truth. One asserts that truth is a correspondence (for example, between a belief and a fact, or an assertion and the reality). The second states that truth consists in demonstrable logical relations with other truths. Here again truth is a kind of relationship, but a coherence rather than a correspondence. Truth comes as a package, as one body. The third theory connects truth with practical value, and so is called the pragmatic theory of truth. Generally, rationalists and idealists see truth as coherence, while empiricists go in for correspondence or the pragmatic theory.

Read about each theory, then try finding its theoretical flaws and drawbacks. Compare your results with the answers provided (not to be taken as the absolute truth!) before going on to the next theory.

Truth as Correspondence

The first theory regards truth as a correspondence between belief and reality. A belief (or a sentence or a proposition) is true just in case it corresponds to the reality it represents. A statement is true if what it says is actually the case, if it represents things the way they stand. If things are as the proposition asserts them to be, then the proposition is true; otherwise not. Falsity consists in a failure of correspondence.

Debate persists as to the nature of this correspondence. On one view, correspondence is a copy, which represents all the elements of the original state of affairs and their interrelationships. The reality is like our true belief in it; it is the way we think it is. But the appearance of yellow (our belief in what yellow looks like) is not a *copy* or *even like* the 570-nanometer light waves that give rise to it. Nor is sweet a copy of sugar.

But a digitized picture exists as stored information on a computer hard drive, even when it is not being viewed. An electronic representation is a correspondence that is no mere copy. Mental representations and sentences can map onto reality in similar abstract ways, so that correspondence becomes shared structure.

The sentence "Such-is-so" has the grammatical structure, *subject-copula-predicate*, which tracks the purported metaphysical structure of the reality, *entity-possession-quality*.

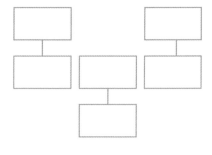

QUESTION 1

What difficulties can you find for the correspondence theory of truth? Play the skeptic and critique it.

Truth as Coherence

The second theory of truth starts from the idea that truth has to make sense—it has to cohere. Preferred by all the great system-builders of philosophy, the rationalists, this theory of truth flows from a conviction that truth is one, that the whole truth is truer than any individual truth, that all truths are interconnected, woven together in one pattern, one world, one system. This system makes sense, it coheres, it hangs together.

In science, the search is to find general laws from which, along with initial conditions, one can logically predict an outcome. Scientific proof uses deduction hypothetically, to derive expected observation from current observations and past regularities. In mathematics, following strict rules of inference, one deduces from axioms or established truths new and unexpected results. Logical interconnectedness arises from ontological interconnectedness. Reason is the Ariadne's thread of truth, the unity leading out of the labyrinth of ignorance.

Ethics, too, makes sense; one ethical principle coheres with another. The coherence of truth in science and mathematics can actually lend strength to the hope that our sense of moral interconnectedness, by which we are bound together on a life-raft earth, is no illusion.

If the world at times seems irrational, indifferent, benignly neutral, that is only because we have not pierced to the moral core, caught the God's-eye glimpse that would make moral sense of the world as certain as mathematical proof.

QUESTION 2

You play the skeptic. Attempt to poke holes in the coherence theory of truth. Sample attempts are provided later in the book.

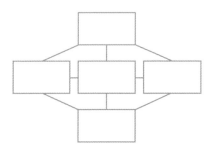

THREE THEORIES OF TRUTH Part 2

Truth as Practical Value

The pragmatic theory of truth identifies truth with the difference a belief makes to experience. Put crudely, truth is what works. More subtly, truth is a process of corroboration and verification, and the ever-updated interim results of this process.

The pragmatist purports to treat truth as experimentalists do. For an experimentalist to give credence to a proposition, it must survive scientific testing. That is, one must make specific predictions based strictly on a precise hypothesis, and then check to see that the predictions all come out true. In short, a hypothesis must make a very definite difference to the ways experiments turn out. This difference to possible experience is the meaning (the cash value, as it were) of the hypothesized proposition. Since truth swings with meaning, truth is just the meaning that pans out, the possible experiences that actually occur.

The pragmatic view is that the meaning of a proposition of science is shown by the methods of its verification, and this must be based on experience. A truth of science is known through the procedures of all the possible experiments that could disconfirm it but don't. If a proposition makes no possible difference to experience, it is utter nonsense, neither true nor false. In the everyday context, the test of practical experience replaces the test of scientific experiment. The meaning of a belief is identified with the consequences of action. Your belief that it is going to rain is inane, unless it leads you to grab an umbrella. What is your belief in God, but your commitment to live according to

God's principles, as you understand them? If you believe in God, but continue your life of sin, you don't really believe. What is your belief in people unless you trust them? Unless belief makes a practical difference in your life, it is for show only. Truth of belief consists in this usefulness.

The pragmatic theory licenses (in special cases only) the will to believe based on emotions, like hope, trust, and love (see Ultimate Choices, pp. 118–119). At issue here are not the verifiable facts of science. The pragmatic theory dispenses with the need to establish a corresponding moral realm, and with the promise of a full and rigorous demonstration through reason alone. Faith can proceed if it bears fruit in a fuller life. *Some things we must believe if they are to be true.* If we all trust each other, we can live peaceably. My belief that we do makes it more true that we do, and makes it more reasonable for others to believe it. Some things we have to believe together for them to be true; we can't all believe unless we each believe.

QUESTION 3

Cast the first philosophical stone. Pick a bone with the pragmatic theory. Some further assaults are provided later in the book for comparison with yours.

ANSWERS

Question 1

Four sample critiques—not necessarily all true!

1. Moral truths correspond to no observable facts. A lie is an observable event; its wrongness is not.
2. To what do mathematical truths correspond? Is there a Platonic Heaven of invisible numbers that correspond to our numerals? To verify our mathematical beliefs, we calculate or construct a proof. We do not look at actual numbers to see if our beliefs, stated in numerals, correspond.
3. If our perceptual beliefs are our representations of the world, and if we only know the world through our representations, how can we check whether our representations correspond to reality or not? It is as if we are told that apples correspond to oranges, but all we ever have are apples.
4. Correspondence theory assumes that human grammar cuts nature at its joints. It imposes grammatical order on reality.

Question 2

1. The coherence theory can't get off the ground. If truths are what may be deduced from other truths, whence the original truths? Proofs must start somewhere. To avoid an infinite regress there must be some non-deduced truths. But the self-evident is empty tautology where it isn't an illusion.
2. Belief systems are incommensurable. To whose belief system must we cohere? To the majority's? To the experts? To your own conscience? Coherence is not enough.

3. The world doesn't make as much sense as is assumed. It is a patchwork quilt of explanations, not all well tied together. No one system can comprehend the whole. There are more ways in heaven and earth than are dreamt of in the coherentist philosophy, despite its rationalist boasts.
4. A one-world ethics system is imperial. One culture's reasonable connection is another culture's violent objection. People consult feelings to settle ethical questions, not logical proof. Reason needs to negotiate with "the unreasonable" toward truth, not deduce it unilaterally with authoritarian certainty.

Question 3

1. The pragmatic theory is *ruthless*. It reduces truth to what is expedient. Truth becomes all too human.
2. The pragmatic theory is *truthless*. It leads to epistemic anarchy. It implies that anything goes: Truth is whatever works for you. But if anything can be true, nothing is true.
3. The pragmatic theory is *toothless*. It is circular. The truth of the pragmatic theory of truth does not satisfy its own criterion. No possible experience could prove it false. It cannot be corroborated.
4. Some truths are *useless*. The pragmatic theory truncates mathematics, limiting it to merely constructive or effective procedures. The real-number continuum and Cantor's Paradise (see pp. 164–165), in particular, are trans-pragmatic.

David Hume

Hume drew an important distinction between kinds of truths and the ways we can know them. He distinguished "relations of ideas" we could know *a priori* (that is, any proposition whose negation is a self-contradiction) from "matters of fact" we could only determine empirically (i.e., with the aid of the senses).

Among the former are all mathematical propositions and all tautologies (see Chapter 4). They can be known *a priori*, which means independently of any testimony of the senses. Matters of fact, by contrast, involve empirical claims involving existence (rather than only logical consistency).

THE COUNTER-PROBLEM OF COUNTER-INDUCTION

Induction has always worked in the past, so it should still work now. The problem is that this reasoning is itself inductive. It would be viciously circular to use induction to prove induction.

To see this problem in a clearer light, consider the principle of counter-induction. *Counter-induction* is a form of reasoning opposite to induction. It is illustrated by the Gambler's Fallacy.

After a long unlucky streak, a losing gambler may come to feel that his turn is due, that his luck will change with the next roll of the dice. The long string of losses he has suffered is so unlikely that he is bound to start winning very soon. The general principle here is counter-inductive: what has not worked in the past will suddenly start to work.

You will object to this as madness and point out that this sort of reasoning has never been known to work. But perhaps its time has come! If induction can prove induction, then why can't counter-induction prove counter-induction?

The Problem of Induction

The sun has risen every day in Earth's history. You'd think that would be reason enough to conclude that it will rise tomorrow. Odds are, it will. But the opposite is possible. No self-contradiction is implied if for some reason before tomorrow the sun goes out. We do not know *a priori* that it will rise. It remains logically possible that it will not, even assuming a past of infinitely many sunrises. What was can never prove what will be. Induction confers no certainty.

A set of facts about yesterday proves nothing about today. Equally, a set of facts past and present proves nothing about the future. Inductive reasoning presumes that what has usually been the case will continue usually to be the case.

Hume also applied his skeptical critique to causal reasoning. Causes are presumed to necessitate their effects, not merely to be regularly conjoined with them. But the senses deliver matters of fact, never necessities. Despite our expectation to the contrary, there is no self-contradiction in the cause occurring (cue ball violently strikes a colored ball) and the effect not occurring (colored ball remains motionless on the billiard table).

How Reason Became a Tool

Hume demoted reason to what is known as *instrumental reason*. He reversed Plato's (political) metaphor that reason should rule over desire and the passions. This was Plato's image of a well-regulated soul, a just soul (see pp. 104–105).

Hume, on the contrary, said that "Reason is a slave to the passions," and must be by its nature. Reason has no motive power. The job and function of reason is to adjudicate among alternative means to a given end by determining which arrives at the goal most efficiently. Of itself, reason cannot determine our ends; passion alone does that for us.

Reason can also help to calculate, among competing goals, what the costs and outcomes of each would be; but it is impotent to pronounce which is better, unless it can learn from our feelings which set of consequences we prefer. Reason is not a check or balance on our passions, not a governor over desires, but only an instrument or means to our satisfaction.

"Ought Begot of Is" Is Illegitmate

Hume is often credited with exposing the *Is–Ought Fallacy*, an illicit but common inference in moral reasoning (see pp. 132–133). The point here, in brief, is that no set of facts can suffice to prove any moral principle. Nothing prescriptive follows from mere description. Ethical necessity cannot be derived from empirically known facts, however extensive. That is not to say that fact is irrelevant to morality, only that what *is* has no authority to establish what *ought to be*. Hume puts it as a logical principle: "From what is, what was, or what will be, it does not follow what ought to be."

The Is–Ought Fallacy is an epistemic point. The fact–value distinction is metaphysical. Both pertain to ethics, our next subject.

Chapter

Ethics and Morality

What it means to be morally right, and what sense
if any can be ascribed to the category of evil, are
questions that have always and quite properly
provoked philosophical inquiry, and in this chapter
we briefly sample ethical styles and theories from
East and West, from ages past and present.
Distressing ethical dilemmas, and other abstract or
all-too-real scenarios fraught with moral meaning,
abound in this chapter, which also features
inspiring descriptions of ethical ideals and virtues.

For not all moral judgments are negative.

MORAL DILEMMAS

Go through the statements below, noting those with which you agree. There are no "right" answers, so just go with your feeling in each case.

1. There are no objective moral standards; moral judgments are merely an expression of the values of particular cultures.
2. It is always wrong to take another person's life.
3. Voluntary euthanasia should remain illegal.
4. There exists an all-powerful, loving, and good God.
5. World War II was a just war.
6. Having made a choice, it is always possible that one might have chosen otherwise.
7. The government should not permit the sale of health treatments that have not been tested for efficacy and safety.
8. There are no objective truths about matters of fact; "truth" is always relative to particular cultures and individuals.
9. Alternative and complementary medicine is as valuable as mainstream medicine.
10. To allow an innocent child to suffer needlessly when one could easily prevent it is morally reprehensible.
11. Individuals have sole rights over their own bodies.
12. Acts of genocide stand as a testament to man's ability to do great evil.
13. The holocaust is a historical reality, taking place more or less as the history books report.
14. The future is fixed. How one's life unfolds is a matter of destiny.

CONCLUSIONS

Now look at the paragraphs below. If you have ticked both numbered statements in any of these cases, you have a moral dilemma. Either there is a contradiction between the two beliefs, or some sophisticated reasoning is required to enable both beliefs to be held consistently. You should either give up one of the two beliefs or find some rationally coherent way of reconciling them.

Statements 1 and 12: Is Morality Relative?

On the one hand, you are saying that morality is just a matter of culture and convention, but on the other, you are prepared to condemn acts of genocide as "evil." Are you willing to say, therefore, that an act of genocide is evil from the point of view of your culture but not evil from the point of view of the culture that is perpetrating it?

Statements 4 and 10: Is There an All-Good, All-Powerful God?

These two beliefs together generate what is known as "The Problem of Evil." The problem is simple: If God is all-powerful, loving, and good, that means he can do what he wants and will do what is morally right. But surely this means that he would not allow an innocent child to suffer needlessly, as he could easily prevent it.

Philosophy: Adventures in Thought and Reasoning

Yet he does. Much infant suffering is the result of human action, but much is also due to natural causes, such as disease, flood, or famine. In all cases, God could stop it, yet he does not.

Statements 8 and 13:
Are There Any Absolute Truths?

If truth is relative, then nothing is straight-forwardly "true" or "factual." Everything is "true for someone" or "a fact for them." So what can you say to those who deny that the holocaust is a fact? Are they not as entitled to their view as you are to yours? How can one both assert the reality of the holocaust and deny that there is a single truth about it?

Statements 3 and 11:
Can I Make Choices For My Own Body?

Why, if individuals have sole rights over their own bodies, should voluntary euthanasia be illegal? You may try to resolve this by saying that the involvement of a third party makes this a special case. However, if I want a tattoo, I need third-party assistance, but this doesn't mean I don't have sole right to decide whether or not I am tattooed.

Statements 2 and 5:
Is Killing Always Wrong?

It is clear here that you must either give up the idea of a just war or get rid of the "always" in the principle "It is always wrong to take another person's life." It is actually very difficult to add to this principle a clause that starts "except," so that it both allows in the kind of killing many feel is justified, yet keeps out the kind of killing that is felt to be unjustified.

Statements 6 and 14:
Is the Future Fixed?

Most people think that humans have free will, and yet many of the same people believe in fate, or destiny. How can both beliefs be true? If "What will be, will be" no matter what we do, then how can we have freedom? If one believes in fate or destiny, then the outcome of our choices is inevitable, and genuine choice is an illusion. This makes it untrue that "Having made a choice, it is always possible that one might have chosen otherwise."

Statements 7 and 9:
What Should be Legal?

Most alternative and complementary medicines have not been tested in trials as rigorously as "conventional" medicine, so why do you believe alternative medicines and treatments need not be as extensively tested as conventional ones? The fact that they use natural ingredients is not in itself good reason, as there are plenty of naturally occurring toxins. Even if one argues that their long history shows them to be safe, that is not the same as showing them to be effective. This is not to criticize alternative therapies, but to question the standards that are used to judge them compared to mainstream medicine.

MORAL CHOICES

In small ways, moral dilemmas confront us all from time to time. We find ourselves faced with choices in which, whatever course of action we take, we must either do something that seems wrong to achieve good, or do the right thing and produce a bad outcome. Which is more important: doing the right thing or having a good result? Can the ends justify the means, whatever they may be, or should we always do the right thing regardless of the consequences? In real-life situations, the relevant factors are rarely clear-cut, but many philosophers have invented scenarios that do away with the gray areas and highlight a black-and-white moral choice, in order to examine the issues that it raises. Here are some classic examples.

EXPERIMENT 1:

You are a pilot in the air force, and the enemy has occupied your country. Your mission is to bomb the town in which they have established headquarters. You understand the need to do this despite the fact that civilians will die in the raid. If you refuse the mission, someone else will do it, but you are ideally qualified because you know the area well—your family lives in that town. Can you do it? Does the importance of the cause outweigh your repugnance at the mission?

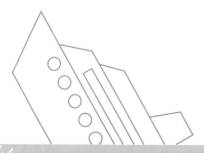

EXPERIMENT 2:

You are the captain of a ship that has sunk. Thirty people are crowded into a lifeboat that can only carry 20, and it will sink unless you do something. You reason that it is better for a few to die than for everyone to do so and, since you know that the boat will need to be rowed if it is to reach safety, you throw the 10 weakest people overboard. When the boat reaches safety, you are tried for murder. How would you expect the jury to view your actions? Would the moral issues have been different if you had prevented the last 10 people from boarding the lifeboat in the first place?

Now consider the entire world as the shipwreck. The cause is worldwide unsustainable development, including human population growth. According to ecologist Garrett Hardin (1974), as the tragedy of the global commons deepens,

Jean-Paul Sartre visiting Berlin in 1948.

the rich nations face the stark choice of those in the lifeboat, fending off the poor nations in the swim who are just clamoring for their fair share. Is the right thing to do to keep our resources for ourselves, or to admit the coming waves of environmental refugees? Or would that only sink our lifeboat? What do you think?

EXPERIMENT 3:

Jean-Paul Sartre provided an example of a thorny dilemma faced by a student who came to him for advice during World War II. The man's brother had been killed by the Germans, and it was his fervent wish to join the war effort, avenge his brother's death, and help to free France, but he lived at home with his ailing mother and knew that she needed him. Which should take precedence: the big issue of the war, in which his contribution may be very small, or a family responsibility that only he can fulfill? How can we decide which of two clashing *prima facie* duties ought to prevail?

In this case, there are good moral reasons for the one remaining son to go, and there are good moral reasons for him to stay. One cannot say he has a duty to do both, since doing both is impossible. But the fact that he can't take both courses of action doesn't mean there aren't equally

compelling moral reasons for him to do each. In this kind of situation, when we have to break one moral requirement or the other, it may seem morally arbitrary which we pick, but pick we must. In part, the problem here is the comparison of goods (duty to one's mother and national service) that are, or appear to be, incommensurable. The one cannot be expressed in terms of the other.

EXPERIMENT 4:

Let us suppose there has been a major earthquake, and thousands of people have been injured. You are in overall control of medical resources, but several hospitals have been destroyed, few qualified medical personnel are available, and medical supplies are limited. You cannot help all the casualties, and it's up to you to produce guidelines that will determine who will receive treatment.

Which of these options do you choose?

1. Refuse treatment to anyone over the age of 70 on the basis that people with more of their life remaining will benefit more.

2. Treat only those with the most serious injuries, reasoning that their need is greatest and the less injured may survive anyway.

3. Treat only those with less serious injuries, because you can treat more of them with your limited resources, and the more seriously injured may die anyway, despite medical intervention.

THE PRISONERS' DILEMMA

Game theory is used in the study of situations in which individuals make choices intended to maximize their benefits, and it can throw light on fields as diverse as economics, evolution, and the nuclear arms race. Crucially, it can help us to understand what constitutes a rational decision when the choices of other "players" affect the outcome but cannot be accurately predicted.

Imagine a situation in which you and an accomplice have committed a crime and you've both been caught. You are being held separately by the police. You are told that if you say nothing and your partner in crime does the same, you'll each receive a six-month prison sentence. If you both tell the police everything, you'll each go to prison for two years. If you spill the beans and your partner says nothing, you'll go free and he'll spend ten years in prison, but if he tells all and you remain silent, you'll get the long sentence. In this scenario, to say nothing is to co-operate with your partner, while informing the police is betraying him. The possible combinations of decisions, and their outcomes, can be shown in a table.

What do you do? Most importantly, what do you think he'll do? Make your choice before reading on.

This example is known as the Prisoners' Dilemma. Since your aim is to minimize your sentence, then unless you can be certain that he will cooperate (which you can't), your best bet is to betray him and avoid the possibility of a ten-year sentence. You might even go free. The likely outcome is that they betray each other and both go to jail for two years.

Decisions	He co-operates	He betrays
You cooperate	You each serve six months	You serve ten years; he goes free
You betray	He serves ten years; you go free	You each serve two years

But what happens if your standpoint is not totally selfish, and you both try to minimize your *joint* sentence? In this case, the logical decision is for you both to cooperate. Neither of you will go free, but your joint sentence is just one year, compared with an average of eight years if either of you betrays. The dilemma is that by cooperating you are both better off, but the rational course for each of you is to betray. In the "iterated" Prisoners' Dilemma, in which the "game" is repeatedly played, players can effectively "punish" each other for betrayal, and cooperation can then emerge as the best strategy.

The Tragedy of the Commons

The Prisoners' Dilemma bears a striking resemblance to the Tragedy of the Commons, a scenario that pits individual rationality against coerced cooperation, claiming only the latter can prevent collective ruin. The tragedy potentially threatens us any time there is open access to a finite common resource, such as: a lake surrounded by lakeside homeowners; pastureland shared by herders; National Forests or other natural amenities open to the public; the fisheries in international waters; even the very air that we all breathe.

In these all-too-real situations, "players" have an incentive to co-operate, but only if others do as well. Each rancher with access to shared grazing land has rational grounds to introduce one more animal, since the benefit at market time of the larger herd is greater than the extra cost of grazing, which is shared. This holds true of every rancher who shares access, and for every additional cow. Following this inexorable logic, the outcome is inevitable overgrazing, and the destruction of the commons.

So long as a commons remains accessible to all, the tendency of rational agents to maximize their individual net benefit will overwhelm the resource, destroying it for all. Only coerced cooperation can optimize the outcome. The problem is how.

PROBLEM:

Imagine a number of people inhabiting the shores of a large lake, with everyone taking their drinking water from it, catching the fish for food, and emptying their waste into the waters. While their numbers are small, the lake can sustain them. But if their population continues to grow, eventually the whole lake will be polluted, the fish stocks will decline, and the water will be undrinkable. Each individual must reduce their consumption, but this will only work if the others do the same.

SOLUTION:

One could divide the lake up and create private property. Each person then has a specific portion of the resource and, theoretically, an incentive to conserve, but in an instance like this—or the case of the atmosphere or the oceans—where the actions of each affects all, this doesn't work.

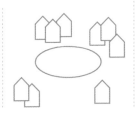

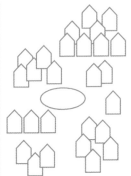

THE GOLDEN RULE

As the basis of a moral code, this Golden Rule, as it is known, has an impressive pedigree, being found in different forms in Hinduism, Buddhism, Confucianism, Judaism, Christianity, Islam, Sikhism, and many other sources. It demands consistency, compassion, and empathy in our social dealings. It is a positive injunction to do good in the world, and in its negative form ("Don't do what you wouldn't like done to you") it proscribes doing of harm. But is the Golden Rule enough, and what are its limitations?

> "Do unto others as you would have them do unto you."

Love Your Neighbor

In the Old Testament commandment to love your neighbor as yourself, the word for "neighbor" is close to that for "kinsman," implying that the rule does not apply to our treatment of those who are different from us; but in the teachings of Jesus (for example, in the parable of the Good Samaritan), it is clear that we must treat all people as equal. This egalitarian edict necessarily ignores the issues of social relationships and status that are a part of everyday life, and which sometimes make it inappropriate to treat others as we would like to be treated.

Personal Choice

Curiously, despite its claim to universality, the Golden Rule places the determination of what is moral in the hands of the individual, since it asks us to act in accordance with our personal standards rather than any universal principle. For example, whereas Kant's concept of the categorical imperative makes lying morally wrong at all times and under all circumstances, the Golden Rule may prompt us to tell other people what we believe they would like to hear.

What If They Wouldn't Like It?

Taking extreme examples, would it be morally right for someone who wishes to die to kill others? Or would a masochist be justified in inflicting physical suffering on others? A codicil, sometimes referred to as the Silver Rule, extends the Golden Rule to read "Treat others as you would wish to be treated *if you were in the other person's position*." This requires us to see the world from the other person's perspective, taking into account his or her personal tastes and cultural or religious background, and to do what is right for them. This form of cultural relativism brings it own problems (see the next page).

Why Act Justly?

In Book 2 of his *Republic*, Plato has his character Glaucon put forward the view that the natural course of action for the individual is not to be just but to commit an injustice—taking what is not ours, for example—as this brings the most benefit. Glaucon proposes that we act justly only because we fear that otherwise others will act unjustly toward us—a somewhat inverse formulation of the Golden Rule.

The Ring of Gyges

To support his proposition, Glaucon recounts the tale of Gyges, a shepherd in the service of the king of Lydia, who finds a marvelous ring that confers invisibility upon the wearer. In short order, Gyges uses the power of the ring to enter the palace, seduce the queen, kill the king, and usurp the throne. Plato's speaker suggests that if a just and an unjust man were each to possess such a ring, they would both use it to commit injustices, and that anyone who acted otherwise would be a fool.

THOUGHT EXPERIMENT

It has been said that a person's moral worth can be measured by what he or she would do if no one ever found out. Suppose you find a lottery ticket and discover that it's worth a fortune. No one will ever know that the ticket was not yours. How do you act?

Option 1. It's wrong to steal: You contact the lottery board, explain the situation, and do all you can to discover the rightful owner.

Option 2. It depends what you do with the money: You claim the winnings and donate the money to worthy causes.

Option 3. Finders keepers: You claim the money and live a life of luxury.

If you choose option 1, then you see eye to eye with Kant (see pp. 66–67).

If option 2, you may have a utilitarian view of right and wrong (see pp. 68–69).

Option 3 is the course of action that Plato's Glaucon would predict (see above).

MORAL RELATIVISM

Ethics is about the right and the good. But a problem arises because people differ profoundly—sometimes diametrically—in what they consider to be right and good. Individuals show variation, and whole cultures and societies also differ. The question is: whose right is right? Or is everyone's conception of good equally good?

This is the problem raised by moral relativism. It seems arrogant, even authoritarian, to set one value system above all the rest. But if everyone is equally right, then it doesn't matter at all what you feel, think, or do. However absurd or bizarre your belief or cultural practice is, if it is just as legitimate as the next guy's, you can do no wrong. The relativity of values appears to force us into a dilemma: dictatorship or anarchy; absolutism or nihilism. Not a pretty choice. But can you define a middle ground? Take a moment to try, before reading on.

Relativity vs. Subjectivity

Different people(s) have different values: this is the (cultural) *relativity* of values. From these facts, no normative statement follows. For instance, it does not follow that every value system is equally true or equally valid. People may have a right to their value beliefs, but that does not make them true, any more than having a right to your opinion makes your opinion true. Also, although some values are relative, others are widely shared.

The *subjectivity* of values consists in values arising from the experiences of individuals. To be a value is just to be a value *for a subject*; in effect, to be a value is to be valued. There are no values without valuers. (Incidentally, this does not prevent a valuer from valuing something *for its own sake*, rather than for the sake of any benefit it may bring to the valuer.)

Importantly, the subjectivity of values does not entail that values are arbitrary. Despite subjectivity, people hold reasons for the values they feel. And despite relativity, people can enter into dialogue with each other about values and reason toward mutual accommodation. People do not stake their identity on arbitrary values, but on issues that are widely recognized to be important. It is often possible to understand those we disagree with, but it takes effort and commitment.

Euthyphro

In Plato's dialogue *Euthyphro*, Socrates confronts a man regarding his views about piety or righteousness. Euthyphro must be an expert, Socrates admits, since he has brought charges of impiety against his own father. Socrates presses him for a definition (*logos*), and does not settle for the examples given to illustrate. So Euthyphro defines the Good as what the gods love. In reply Socrates asks: Is the Good good because the gods love it, or do the gods love it because it is good? Put differently, is what is right the arbitrary whim of divine authority? Or is divine authority backed by reason, and not merely power?

There is a similar question tuned to our democratic age. Is a government action right because people demand it (as per "anything goes" relativism)? Or do people demand it because it is right (for example, due to their fundamental decency)?

YOU OR ME?

The short one says to the tall one, "If I were you, I'd be tall." The tall one replies, "No, if you were me, I'd be short."

How could you? How would you feel if someone did that to you? If you would feel wronged, why shouldn't they? If you would have a right to object, so do they!

Thus we chide others, and are ourselves chided, when we act in a selfish or negligent way, causing harm to others (sometimes without even realizing it). The principle of equality is backed up with an indirect appeal to personal experience. This self-reflection may be painful and unwelcome at first, but sometimes our imaginative leap persuades us, and we make amends and change behavior. The principle of equality is backed up with an indirect appeal to personal experience.

Whatever good such self-reflection does in the world, one can wonder whether it doesn't get the issue back to front. Perhaps it would be better for us to imagine—not ourselves in the position of the other—but what it is like for others being who they are. Rather than imagining ourselves in their position, perhaps we should imagine (if we can) their position as they see it. It is not enough to see the world through their eyes; we must see their world.

We can walk a mile with someone, or we can walk a mile in his or her shoes. The latter is likely to be the more painful option, but also more conducive to mutual understanding and peaceful resolution of conflict.

Our personal feelings are a potential source of bias. People may not feel the way that we do. Should our own self and feelings set the moral standard, or should we drop the self and raise the other up on their terms? I think you should decide.

FOUR META-ETHICAL PERSPECTIVES

Getting Down to Basics

Philosophies of ethics vary in many respects. They may disagree on particular cases or on matters of principle. When philosophies clash over what to do in a particular instance, what is really at stake is often some principle or other. So far in this chapter we have explored controversial cases and touted principles.

But it also sometimes happens that we agree on the morally required action in a specific case, but disagree as to why. What makes something right for you is not what makes it right for me, even when we agree that it is right. There is general and public accord that theft, lying, cheating, breaking promises, and vandalism are wrong. But they seem wrong to different people for different reasons: they are impractical; the risk of punishment is too high; they are sins; one wouldn't want them to happen to oneself; they are inconsistent with other goals we value more highly; some are prohibited by laws enacted by legitimate authorities; or we feel that they degrade our souls and consider them beneath our dignity. The language used shows the sort of reasoning involved.

Four Foundations: Virtue, Right, Utility, Care

Over the next few pages, you will be able to explore four such philosophies, four contrasting styles of ethical reasoning, four distinct frameworks used for making moral sense of the world. Each is characterized by taking a certain moral concept as its fundamental cornerstone: virtue, right,

utility, or care. As mere concepts, this list contains no logical inconsistency. But the worldviews associated with each concept taken as trump are decidedly in conflict, not only over cases and principles, but over priorities and perceptions.

The four meta-ethical philosophies to be covered are alive and well, operative in most of us in some degree or other due to cultural inheritance. But they can also be seen (very crudely) in historical succession. Virtue-based theories characterize many of the great ancient philosophies. Rights-based thinking, though it does not originate in modern times, is broadly characteristic of the early rise of liberal democracies and thinking about individual rights. Over the last two centuries, utilitarianism adopted its contemporary forms and held sway in policy circles and personal consciences.

The care-based ethic has no doubt existed as long as care itself; its like is discernible in the words of Jesus and the Buddha. But in recent times it has often been articulated in the context of feminist critiques of male-dominated and male-biased ethical theory. Here ethical theory is separated to the extent possible from political issues. Even historical differences are papered over and other philosophical disagreements suppressed. The point is simply to give the flavor of each foundational concept, so you recognize the taste of each meta-ethical perspective as it arises in everyday life.

Meta-Ethics as Worldviews

To take one of these four concepts as foundational is to make it integral to one's worldview. In order for the world we live in to be a moral world, it must be interpreted as such. We do this all the time, but not always with philosophical awareness of our own presumptions, the moral lenses we make tacit use of. Familiarity with our meta-ethical options can lead to better self-understanding as we learn to express what is important to us in the most suitable and evocative terms. After you have read all four sections and thought through the critical questions provided on each cornerstone concept, complete the subsequent dinner-table dialogue exercise (pp. 76–77) to test your recognition of the four competing perspectives and contrasting worldviews.

Since increasingly today human beings are driven to take account of our moral relations with the living earth, the four divergent concepts have also been extended from the circle of human concern to the earth and its life-sustaining ecosystem. The section on Ethics and Ecology (pp. 72–75) shows how these concepts may be applied to the philosophical problem of our responsibilities toward the environment.

Virtue: An Ethics of Character
  "Virtue" means excellence.
  Vision: a flourishing happiness
    (eudaimonia).
  Concerns: character (ethos)
    and destiny.

Right: An Ethics of Persons
  "Right" means principled, lawful,
    the inviolable.
  Vision: justice, fairness, autonomy,
    liberty.
  Concerns: duty, dignity, universality,
    choice.

Utility: An Ethics of Experience
  "Utility" means pleasure or
    satisfaction.
  Vision: greatest good for
    greatest number.
  Concerns: consequences, welfare,
    equality.

Care: An Ethics of Difference
  "Care" means empathy.
  Vision: non-coercive relationship,
    peace.
  Concerns: inclusivity, diversity.

Note: Visions are political contenders; but Concerns are **not** exclusive.

The Trolley Problem

THE PROBLEM:

You are standing beside train tracks and see a speeding trolley about to pass you. To your horror, you see that if the trolley continues it will run over five people on the tracks. You also notice a fork in the track, between the people and the trolley. You realize that you can divert the trolley to a different track simply by pulling the lever. If you do, the five will be saved; however, a person standing on the other track will surely die. What should you do?

THE METHOD:

Philosophers have used ethical dilemmas like this one to test their intuitions and build a better ethical theory. Here is your chance to try. Start with your gut reaction to this case. If you are like most people (and empirical studies of opinions have been conducted), you would say that the best of a bad situation is to pull the lever, divert the trolley, kill the one but spare the five. (If you are unlike most people, and have a different opinion, the method will work for you as well.) Your first impression (whatever it is) as to what to do has the status of an intuition regarding a particular case. For this intuition to be ethically correct, there must be some general ethical principle which would warrant it. Your objective is to articulate such a principle that lends logical and ethical justification to your intuitive conclusion, then to test your newfound principle against other cases.

For instance, you might well respond to this demand for general ethical reasons supporting your intuition by noting simply that killing one person to save five lives is clearly a better consequence than letting five die for the sake of the one. The underlying principle here clearly points to the *consequences* of our actions: we should always act so as to maximize the beneficial (and minimize the harmful) consequences of our actions. This is a version of the Greatest Happiness Principle. Notice that the principle is perfectly general, in contrast to the special circumstances of the particulars of the trolley problem, to which we are applying the general rule.

If you are in the minority, you might have come up with a justifying principle to the effect that it is always wrong to take an innocent person's life, even though you must sometimes let bad things happen to avoid doing so. This argument, and the previous ones, cannot both be sound; they are meant here only to illustrate the method you are to apply to your own intuition. You may have come up with very different arguments than these to support your initial intuitive conclusion. Notice that, in either case, the ethical warrant for the action comes in the form of a general principle. Typically, one recommends a particular action as the correct one in a given scenario based on ethical standards that apply generally. Formulate the ethical norm your chosen action follows before going on.

THE SOLUTION:

To test your intuitive answer, let's check if your general premise always applies. Imagine a similar situation to the trolley problem just described, except that this time the lever works differently. Also different, you are no longer beside the tracks; you are standing on a footbridge over the tracks. You see the trolley hurtling toward the five innocents. The only way you can spare them all from a terrible fate is to block the train in its path; but the only nearby object large enough to block the train is an innocent portly fellow standing beside you on a trapdoor in the footbridge. (You yourself, we may assume, are too slight even to slow the speeding trolley by leaping in its path.) In this case, if you pull the lever, the trapdoor will open, and the rotund bystander will fall into the trolley's path. He will surely die, but the five on the track will be saved. The consequences in terms of numbers of death (or greatest happiness) are exactly the same as in the previous case. Thus if it is your duty in the previous case to pull the lever (killing one to rescue five), you ought in the present case do the same to the big guy.

If you are like most people, you balk at pulling the lever in the second case, though it will save five innocent lives, but not at saving those same lives by pulling a lever in the first case (though it may even be the same large man on the alternate tracks). Your challenge has now become: how to adjust your judgment, or your ethical principle, to restore ethical consistency; or, failing that, to discern in the two cases some *ethically relevant difference* that makes it right in one case, wrong in another, to kill one in order to save five. The latter is made difficult by the fact that the only difference between the two cases (the lever mechanism) is ethically irrelevant.

Test your ethical principles further by considering one more case. Suppose you are a transplant surgeon with five dying patients, each with a different failing organ. One healthy person arrives at your office who, you realize, his kidneys are a perfect match for one of your patients, his liver perfectly suits another, his heart could save another of your patient's lives, and so on. You realize that, in terms of consequences, in order to minimize suffering and maximize healthy lives, the optimal course of action is a painless death for the stranger, and the equitable distribution of his life-saving organs.

The minority view mentioned above might seem to fare better in these last two scenarios. If it is always wrong to take an innocent life, then it is wrong to push the fat man over the bridge or harvest the organs of the one for the great happiness of the many. Still the principle in question does lead to a difficult result in the original case, where five innocents are let die to save one innocent.

VIRTUE: AN ETHICS OF CHARACTER

Excellence is a synonym for virtue. A virtue-based ethics is interested in excelling, in superlative functioning, and in achieving much and greatly. It is concerned with realizing our full potential. It wants not simply to get things done, but to get them done well, and to aim at the best—or better.

The final goal of virtue-based ethics is a vision of being all we can be. Having a final goal, virtue-based ethics is called teleological. (The Greek word *telos* means "end" or "purpose.") Within the framework of virtue, ethical reasoning is directed toward the realization of esteemed ends, and seeks to ensure that our purpose here is served in all we do.

Virtue is to be distinguished from honor, which must be bestowed upon us by others.

Honor is a matter of reputation, whereas virtue depends on your track record, your history of actual accomplishments, your deeds good or ill. Virtue must be won by good conduct, usually through struggle with our lesser natures.

Virtue is not duty. On the contrary, it is above and beyond the call of duty. Virtues are not strictly necessary, but rare and exceptional accomplishments, worthy of emulation and challenging to surpass. They are not unconditional obligations, but inspiring ideals that lead us on, ever better.

Our ultimate purpose, the realization of all the best in human potential, is known both as flourishing and as eudaimonia. The latter term comes from a Greek word that is often translated as "happiness," but which more literally means "good-spirited" or "fortunate." Such wellbeing is not felt as mere pleasure, however intense, whether fleeting or prolonged. Rather, it is experienced as self- and collective actualization, as a full and complete

VIRTUE QUESTIONS

Is this who I want to be?

Is this the best we can be (or do)?

Will this policy promote the kind of community we want to live in?

What are our best purposes?

life, as exceptional greatness, as nothing less than a blessed existence. The reward of the heroes of virtue is the unforgettable glory of the Elysian Fields, or an afterlife amid the stars.

As this suggests, not all virtues are ethical in nature. Excellence may be demonstrated in numerous fields of endeavor. One can speak of military, athletic, musical, civic, or spiritual virtues. There are pragmatic virtues, even bureaucratic virtues, but also epistemic and scientific ones. But the general notion of superlative functioning has its most significant application in the ethical domain, and in this way a general worldview (or teleology) puts its stamp upon ethical reasoning. Put differently, a conception of the Good Life is presupposed, then superimposed upon ethical thinking.

Ethical virtues are the qualities or traits of good character. Virtue-based ethics is very much an ethics of character, aimed at excellence in personal conduct and interpersonal dealings. Good character consists of those personality attributes that best subserve individual and collective flourishing. As ethical traits, virtues manifest themselves as the knowledge,

habits, or actions that determine a person's moral quality, judged from the standpoint of the preconceived Good Life.

Theories of virtue differ. Socrates directly equated virtue and knowledge—namely, self-knowledge. The unexamined life was a life without virtue, hence a life without worth. Such Socratic intellectualism is reflected in Plato's definition of courage as the knowledge of what to fear. Aristotle, by contrast, conceived of virtue as a habit, that is, as a learned tendency or predisposition for appropriate feelings and actions. A habit is a state of character, not a state of knowledge. Confucius identified reciprocal virtues conducive to basic social relationships (for example, husband–wife, father–son, ruler–subject). Each reflected in its own way the primary Confucian virtue humaneness, or human-heartedness, but they worked together serving social harmony.

For four spiritual virtues, see pp. 80–81.

CRITICAL THINKING QUESTIONS

Give some examples of **(a)** athletic, **(b)** epistemic, **(c)** bureaucratic, **(d)** musical, and **(e)** scientific virtues.

ANSWERS

(a) Sportsmanship, fair play, teamwork

(b) Perspicacity, acumen, rationality, wit, depth, balance, impartiality

(c) Efficiency, political neutrality, loyalty, accountability, transparency, tact

(d) Rhythm, sense of pitch, timing, soul

(e) Observance, rigor, inferential caution, respect for fact, economy of assumption

Aristotle's Ethics

For Aristotle, ethics is a science to be pursued not in order to acquire knowledge for its own sake, but to acquire knowledge that will guide action. In all action and inquiry, we aim at some good. Some things we want in order to obtain something else (like money for food); other things we want for their own sake (such as pleasure, health, and happiness). While we want pleasure and health for their own sake, they are not self-sufficient; that is, we also want them in order to be happy. Happiness, however, is self-sufficient. Everything else is done or desired for the sake of happiness, but happiness is desired only for its own sake. Thus Aristotle's ethics is *teleological*, aimed at the realization of inherent purposes of human life. The *telos* is flourishing (= *eudaimonia*).

How to Live

The question of the best way to conduct oneself in life now becomes a matter of determining which course of action promotes true human happiness. Aristotle's conclusion is that, in order to be happy, one has to live a life of virtue, not as a means to an end, but as the realization of that end. Flourishing requires human excellence, the fullest possible realization of fundamental human capacities (such as friendship, deliberation, association, civic life, and knowledge). Humans are social animals, so our flourishing is social as well. Civic or social virtues can only be developed in association with others, in a community or city-state (the Greek word is *polis*), through education.

Virtue Is a Habit

For Aristotle, then, happiness is activity of the soul in accordance with virtue. Human happiness is life lived in accord with virtue. But what is virtue? Is it knowledge, a feeling, a choice, or a habit? For Aristotle, virtue is a settled habit, a character trait, a state or disposition of the soul. Ethical virtues are traits of good character. They involve choice, but Aristotle does not pretend to offer a method by which to always choose rightly. They concern our feelings as well, since action so often springs from desire and passion. Essentially, virtues are dispositions to feel and to act in certain ways.

Virtue does not come by fortune, but by one's own efforts. Misfortune can remove it, but virtue is not a capacity that we are born with. Rather, we must develop it through practice and the right kind of upbringing. Education is vital, especially having virtuous people one can emulate. Virtue is a habit, but it is a cultivated habit that involves appropriate feeling, and requires experience—that is, practice in choosing. A good character is established, not by a single good action, but by continual refinement over a lifetime.

TABLE OF ARISTOTELEAN VIRTUES

Each row indicates an underlying passion (in parenthesis) as well as two character flaws (vices) due to its deficiency or excess. The virtue is the mean, which represents the appropriate or functional degree of passion leading to measured action relative to circumstances.

VICE OF DEFICIENCY	VIRTUE (underlying passion)	VICE OF EXCESS
cowardice	courage (confidence)	rashness (hubris)
insensitivity	moderation (desire for bodily pleasure)	overindulgence
pusillanimity	magnamity (desire for pleasure)	vanity
shamelessness	modesty (shame)	bashfulness
self-deprecation	truthfulness (self-presentation)	boastfulness
surliness	friendliness (desire to please others)	obsequiousness
boorishness	wittiness (desire to amuse others)	buffoonery
spite, gloating	righteous indignation (feeling the (mis)fortunes of others)	envy

RIGHT: AN ETHICS OF PERSONS

Representative Philosophers:
Locke, Rousseau, Kant, Isaiah Berlin, John Rawls.

Sample Rights: The right to life and liberty; the right to hold and sell property; political rights (to vote, to assemble, to protest peaceably); equality rights; freedom of speech and of the press; legal rights (to a lawyer, to know the charges, to face one's accusers, to a trial by jury).

Sample Maxims: Never treat people merely as a means, but always also as an end in themselves. Your right to swing your fist ends at my nose.

What is right is what is principled and just. Fairness is right because it is just. Justice is not merely an excellence of individual conduct. Social arrangements, working conditions, economic distribution, and constitutional agreements may also be just or unjust. It is up to people to realize the opportunities that life affords, but without a level playing field, people don't have a fair shake, and an injustice is done. Peoples' rights are being violated.

A right is essentially a legitimate claim that a person may have. Some rights we acquire in our daily affairs; all it takes is a promise, a handshake, or merely standing in line. Some rights are creatures of contract; others we acquire by virtue of being citizens, such as the right to vote or obtain a passport. But the deepest rights we do not acquire—we hold them simply because we are human beings; we hold them by dint of human dignity. They are inseparable from us without violation. They exist in principle even if they are not recognized or respected.

Fundamental human rights are the inalienable birthright of every person; considerations of sex, skin color, religion, politics, net worth, and pedigree are morally irrelevant. The dignity of the individual is enshrined in this *ethics of persons*, rather than excellence of conduct. Moral respect is owed to all people. The worst of us deserve respect; bad character is no forfeit of human worth. Even those sentenced to death for unconscionable crimes must be treated humanely, despite their having denied the same treatment to others. This universality of rights arguably has a root in the teachings of Jesus, and in the vibrant idea that even the lowest of the low possess basic human worth.

RIGHTS QUESTIONS

Does this action, rule, or policy accord respect to all stakeholders?

Is it universalizable? (Could we all do it?)

Are any stakeholders treated merely as a means?

Do all stakeholders get to participate in deciding? Do they all consent? Is it fair?

simply match or exceed a lofty expectation, nor fulfill some lauded function well. It is never the consequences (function, end, utility) that make an action right, but the principle *behind* the action, the ethical law to which it adheres, the *intention*.

The focus on intention, apart from consequences, relieves this meta-ethical perspective from its stern insistence on duty. Our moral intentions are expressions of our choices, aspects of human will. Freedom takes its place alongside necessity in this framework, not only because liberties are rights, but because the choice of principles to live by defines *moral autonomy*.

A rights-based perspective rejects teleology. It refuses to see ethics as the maximization of a good, whether flourishing or utility. The right thing to do might not coincide with that which most promotes happiness or the greatest good for the greatest number. Your duty is to do the right thing, the principled thing, not to make people happy or attain personal greatness. The rights framework is therefore called *deontological* (from the Greek root *deon*, which means "duty," what is binding or needful).

Right is the basis of duty; it is the call of duty. Individual rights impose necessary constraints on the behavior of others. Your right correlates to the duties of others, which they can never evade on grounds of expediency, general welfare, or the greater good. Your duty is what is morally necessary for you to do, what is mandatory and/or incumbent upon you. Duty implies ethical necessity, a non-negotiable, unshirkable obligation. Dutiful action conforms to principle; it does not

CRITICAL THINKING QUESTIONS

Question 1

If you have a right to vote, do you have a duty to vote? Compulsory voting may be going too far, but is there a moral duty to vote? Do you have a civic virtue or a civic duty?

Question 2

Rights exist in principle, not in fact. None has ever seen a right, or laid a hand on one. They can't be sensed by nose, mouth, or ear. Sense perception gives us matters of fact, never rights or values. On what grounds do you know that rights exist, and which there are?

UTILITY AND PLEASURE

Utility Is the Good

In philosophy, *utility* is a name for anything that produces a benefit or an advantage, pleasure or happiness. It may be the satisfaction of desire or of preference. Whatever is in something's interest is good for that thing, has some utility from its perspective. Not everything has a perspective. Presumably, plants, stones, and bacteria have no inner life. But any sentient being is capable of experiencing pain or pleasure, enjoying a benefit or an advantage, or of being injured or harmed by the actions of others. On the utilitarian view, only that which tends to confer such an experienceable boon is good. All that detracts from utility is evil: such is any loss or disadvantage, any pain, unhappiness, or harm.

The Greatest Good Is Your Duty

Granted the nature of the good lies in the experience of utility, the question remains: How should you behave? What is the right thing to do? The answer is: Do the most good. What you ought to do is ensure that the consequences of your actions produce the greatest happiness for the greatest number. That action is your duty that maximizes the net utility for all those concerned, as compared to the consequences of all the other actions available to you.

Clearly, utilitarianism is *teleological*, rather than deontological. Duty is derived from a principle of overall utility maximization; the right is determined by the good. Since the good in question always concerns the consequences of an action, no action or intention is considered intrinsically right or wrong. The *telos* or end is the greatest possible resulting happiness, not necessarily the most excellent achievement, which makes utilitarian happiness very different from

UTILITY QUESTIONS

What are the consequences in terms of suffering or its converse?

Does any alternative action have a greater net benefit?

Has the interest of every being potentially affected been equally considered?

virtue-induced *eudaimonia*. Utilitarian philosophy will likewise admit the existence of rights, but only if they are derived from its greatest-happiness principle. Thus the utilitarian duty to eliminate gratuitous suffering is tantamount to the individual right of any sentient being not to be harmed in vain.

Do What You Like—Only Cause No Harm!

The flipside of duty is liberty or permission. One may do all that is not forbidden. Utilitarianism forbids only that which causes useless harm, or what foregoes a good for no greater good. The harm principle is a principle of wide liberty: One may live however one likes, as long as one causes no harm to others. This principle is friendly toward diversity in lifestyles, and resists the imposition of any single ideal. The state may intervene in the lives of citizens only to prevent harm to others.

And yet, utilitarianism recognizes that there are costs to doing moral business. Sometimes one takes it on the chin for the good of others, or takes pains to prevent suffering, like swallowing bitter medicine or visiting the dentist. Pain is good if it leads to less pain overall. Utilitarianism may also impose limits to individual rights based on public welfare, collective interests, or the greater good. For the sake of the greater good, no right is inviolable.

Radical Equality of Consideration

If one locates the good in experienceable benefits, only beings capable of experience are relevant to moral considerations. On the other hand, all sentient beings deserve consideration, and that consideration must be full, equal, and impartial. Consideration must be equal for all, but not necessarily respect, since hard decisions might require unequal treatment in cases where the suffering of a few could massively enhance the overall benefits.

Utilitarianism widens the circle of moral concern beyond human beings to any species that can suffer from pain or disutility. This expansion of the morally relevant sphere has major implications for government policy, systems of production, even lifestyle choices.

CRITICAL THINKING QUESTIONS

Question 1
Human Agency: Life guided exclusively by utilitarian principles would only aim at the greatest happiness for the greatest number, and not preferentially serve those near and dear to us. Can personal relationships be conducted on such an impersonal basis? Can agents be neutral?

Question 2
A utilitarian must always do "the least bad thing to prevent the worst thing that would otherwise happen in the circumstances." Do strict utilitarians leave themselves open to blackmail by terrorists?

CARE: AN ETHICS OF RELATIONSHIP

Representative Philosophers:
Carol Gilligan (psychologist),
Nel Noddings, Buddha?, Jesus?

Samples of Care:
Empathy, sympathy, nurturance,
commitment, nursing, tending, being
there for someone.

Sample Maxims:
It is more important to be kind than
right. The personal is political. Commit
random acts of kindness. It takes a
village to raise a child. Each according
to its needs.

The Challenge of Care

Care ethics has only recently been
formulated and expressly advocated.
While it has affinities with the other three
frameworks, it is characterized by its
opposition to perceived biases within them.
It asks: is there not *a net loss to the
personal* amid the abstract principles of
justice, fairness, and duty, or in the
agent-neutral motivation of the ideal
utilitarian? Is there not a greater lesson in
the personal commitment of a simple act
of care? Is it not *useful*, *virtuous*, even our
duty, to cover these bloodless imperatives
of universal reason with a human face?

Reason and Feeling

Unlike the other meta-ethical perspectives,
which seek principles agreeable to reason

and valid for all (or at least for the
virtuous), the stance of care is taken up
within the personal, concrete, particular
relations where we live. It is little
concerned to formulate competing
foundations, and tends at times to eschew
ethical theory altogether. The stance of
care is activist. Care is committed.

Moral viewpoints arise prior to
justification and prior to philosophy.
Care-based ethics is a skeptical challenge
to the dogmatism of reason within ethics,
to the heroic ambition to find an ultimate
theory. But it is no mere feminist gibe, nor
yet the announcement of an exclusively
female mode of being. We all enter into
caring relationships and we need them in
order to grow, learn, teach, and heal.
Reason ought to be man enough to take
the ribbing and reverse the biases of
impartiality and universality, abandon the
pretense of emotionless superiority. Reason
can learn to care.

CARE QUESTIONS

Who is speaking for those who cannot
speak for themselves?

Are these relationships exploitative?

Have the silenced been heard?

Are you safe?

Individuals in Relationships

Care is the partial attention to particular beings, a steady commitment to their present and future wellbeing, extended to each according to its developing needs. Care is room to grow–together. Care is concerned with individual needs, but here the individual is personal, not an abstract equal; and individuals come to be, exist, and fulfill themselves only through caring relationships. This is not the rugged individual, but the *relational* individual. Indeed, the focus shifts from the individual as such to the boundaries between individuals, where the personal and political meet. Care is an aspect of relationship before it is an aspect of the individual.

The image of care is the dedicated gardener, the attentive nurse, the loving mother. The appropriate action is motivated by the situational needs of the garden, the patient, or the child, not by principles like great excellence or duty for duty's sake. Care is as selfless as any impartial utilitarian, but it is not impartial; it is a personal and privileged love. It is not the universal love of humanity. Nor is it the exclusive duty or function of women. To care is no more female than to reason is to be male. Care ethics is anti-essentialist (see Appearance and Reality, pp. 86–87).

An Ethics of Difference

Equality and fairness are central to modern rational ethics. Without attempting to establish opposite principles, the ethics of care highlights *differences* that exist among people, and calls for an ethics that addresses the power inequalities inherent in important relationships, unlikely to be eliminated even if they ought to be. The infant is helpless and needs its parents; the career of the student depends on the grades and approval given by professors; the patient must submit to the doctor. Care needs to go on in these relationships despite the asymmetry, in full respect of differences.

Care and Rainbows

The context of relationship raises the issue of the Other, and challenges us to take the perspective of the Other, to understand others according to their needs. Care is empathy. The acceptance of individual differences broadens to a political vision of inclusivity and non-coercive social relations. Care ethics does not merely tolerate difference—it nurtures diversity. For this, the public, private, and international spheres must be free of domination and exploitation. The demand of care is peace.

CRITICAL THINKING QUESTIONS

Question 1

Is there a duty to care? Can you love another person out of duty? Does the motivation of duty (namely, to do what is ethically necessary) preclude or render inoperative the spontaneous love of the heart?

Question 2

Prolonged over-emphasis on the Other leads to care burnout. How can society care for the caregivers? How can we nurture self-care?

ETHICS AND ECOLOGY

Philosophical ethics has been very largely concerned with the fate of human beings, rather than with our moral relations with the rest of the living world. But not all the values of life are definable in human terms, if only because life itself is not definable in human terms, but includes the web of nature, the ecosphere, the very conditions of life, and of human life. The inconvenient moral truth is that we must learn to widen the circle of our moral concern, and let it encompass the whole earth.

Utility and Ecology

For the utilitarian, the Good is based on pleasure and pain, so the circle of concern naturally extends to all sentient beings. Any human action, institution, or policy that results in pain is evil unless it is indispensable for greater happiness for a greater number of sentient beings. Our moral concern cannot be restricted to those whose rational choice may be infringed, but must extend to any being that may suffer. This includes those with sufficient nervous systems to yield sentient awareness. Bacteria and plants (barring any secret inner life they may lead) are presumably not sentient. Such unfeeling beings can only be relevant to our utilitarian deliberations as means to the ends or purposes of sentient beings. They cannot be ends in themselves, if the principle of utility is taken as exclusively true.

Applied to natural resource extraction, utilitarian views have played a significant role, notably in government use of benefit–cost analysis in development projects. Often utilitarian philosophy is honored in the breach, as when human utilities are exclusively considered. A utilitarian spirit demands *conservation* of resources (for the welfare of future generations), whereas *preservation* of the wild for its own sake does not fit the utilitarian mold. Strictly, the welfare of the forest is of greater importance than the sustainable forest product extracted from it for market (human use). The sentient beings of the forest deserve equal consideration (if not ultimately equal treatment) in the light of a pure, uncorrupted, non-anthropocentric utilitarian ethics.

TESTING THE UTILITY OF RIGHTS

Where do fundamental rights come from? Do they arise from human declarations or historical struggle? Are rights constructed by human societies, or inherent in beings by their very nature? If we are born with rights, why are they not specified in our genes?

Even if restricted to human beings, the principle of equal consideration has profound consequences for issues of sustainable development. Don't future generations deserve exactly the same consideration as do those who, by accident, happen to be alive today? Are we to discount utilities of the future, or offload the costs of our lifestyle onto our progeny? Social planning aimed honestly at maximizing human welfare over the long run would mean a transformation of contemporary policy-making, production systems, and institutional governance.

Ecocentric Rights

The rights-based view rejects sentience as a criterion of moral relevance. Why should the capacity to feel pain and pleasure be the price of respect? What makes life that doesn't feel or experience any less worthy than life that does? A duty of respect is owed to every moral person, irrespective of his or her station in life. But why do we consider human beings the only moral persons? Corporations are granted artificial personhood for legal purposes. Why shouldn't living beings with a real and continuing interest in their own existence be accounted as *natural* persons, with *moral* rights irrespective of their niche in the biosphere?

In terms of an ecocentric rights-based ethics, we owe moral respect to all forms of life—not only to individual specimens, but to living systems as such, like estuaries, watersheds, mountains—most consummately to the earth and its self-regulating ecosphere, the most inclusive concrete moral person of all, nicknamed Gaia.

To grant rights to other species is not necessarily to grant the same rights to all species. Ecocentrism does not imply bioegalitarianism (which *does* uphold the equal inherent right of every species to exist, even gnats, grubs, bacteria, malarial mosquitoes, even useless plants and hideous animals). An ecocentric ethics takes rights-based universalization to a new level, with or without the principle of equality. Corporations cannot speak for themselves, so they hire lawyers who represent their interests in court. Living systems too are mute, so their legal representatives will need to be appointed. Just as infirm or incompetent persons are legally recognized as persons, their interests protected by complex trust law, so too living systems can have legally recognized "friends," advocates who, under trust law, stand for their interests.

Arguably, some rights are held collectively in virtue of the inscrutable interdependencies of life forms. What rights has prey against the predator?

The individualism that is standard in rights-based thinking is inimical to the intricate mutual interdependencies at play in the ecosphere. Collective and competing rights need to be accepted. Even without individualism, the rights framework generally involves an adversarial approach to dispute resolution. As at law and in all politics, struggle, compromise, and sacrifice are indispensable for justice.

The Ecology of Virtue

The concept of "flourishing" (eudaimonia) extends readily to plants and animals, even to ecosystems. All can be said to flourish, to do well (or not). Even if they do not *experience* happiness, they can have a fortunate or less fortunate existence. Flourishing can be understood in a species-specific sense, and the wellbeing of the biotic community is readily conceived as a web of interconnected flourishing.

If virtue is an aspect of the excellent life that is flourishing, virtue too, as a concept, would transfer to the ecological realm. But virtues are normally understood to involve choice, decision, action, and achievement. Does it add anything to knowledge to say that birds that migrate well do so virtuously? In regard to human affairs, however, certain virtues or excellences of conduct, character, or design may indeed serve as useful ideals in the greening of behavior and production. Among the eco-virtues: stewardship; simplicity; forebearance; prudence; precaution; eco-efficiency; avoidance of waste; and economy of design. Walking softly is a virtue.

A virtue-based ethics is teleological, based on a conception of human function and the human good. Since Aristotle, much Western philosophy till Darwin recognized a natural hierarchy of purposes (Great Chain of Being), with human beings at the top. This political elitism is not consistent with the new ecological ideal, in which living beings are nested and interwoven in each other, both means and ends to the life of other living beings. Except at the extremes of biological organization, life lives by consuming life. Humans need to reconceive function and purpose within nature. Human culture and economy—our flourishing—must find a way to exist without impinging on a flourishing ecosphere. We must struggle softly to survive.

Care of the Earth

Local effort is essential in addressing many global environmental problems (think of non-point-source pollution, such as tailpipe emissions and domestic energy waste). Sustainable local food production requires attentive care to the local ecosystem over the long term. Just as care requires care of self, communities must husband their natural resources for renewal and for their own benefits, but only through respectful relations, attending to the needs of the living earth for its own sake.

Human-caused destruction of species and habitat is preventable exploitation. Biophilia is the ecological counterpart of care. Learning to live within the biophysical limits of Gaia requires us to take the perspective of Nature as the cared-for Other. We must find the self in relationship with the land, not through merging or oneness with nature.

Domination over women is conceptually linked to domination of nature. Thus sustainability requires the emancipation of women worldwide. Women are a major consumer group, buying for themselves and their families. The education of girls is a most effective means of population control, without which sustainable development is impossible. Women play a major role, especially in developing countries, in natural resource management, and do more than their global share of agricultural work, whether for subsistence, trade, or wages.

"Women have a vital role in environmental management and development. Their full participation is therefore essential to achieve sustainable development."

—Principle 20 of the UN's Agenda 21

THOUGHT EXPERIMENT

An Ecology of Care
"Care eco-ethics is just cleaning up your own back yard, a form of NIMBY—'not in my backyard.' Care is unprepared to make hard decisions." Is this a valid challenge to eco-ethics?

SPOT THAT META-ETHICAL PERSPECTIVE!

In this exercise, you listen in on an everyday conversation and try to identify the four meta-ethical frameworks when they are evoked. After each contribution to the ethical dialogue, you are asked which ethic is at work. All four of the key concepts are expressed, though none ideally. Do not expect consistency: there may be one or more involved in each speaker.

Dinner-Table Dialogue

One evening at supper, Leslie, aged 14, refuses to eat meat. "If it's wrong to kill people and eat them, it's wrong to kill animals and eat them."

QUESTION 1

Which meta-ethical concept is implicit in Leslie's moral reasoning?

Robert, her 16-year-old brother, makes a show of enjoying his hamburger. "You talk about moral consistency, yet you are wearing leather shoes. If it's OK to kill animals and wear them, maybe you would look good in a pair of human-skin shoes."

QUESTION 2

What core moral concepts does Robert use here?

Leslie replies: "Gross!" Her father John intervenes. "He has a point. Eating or wearing it, either way an animal was killed for our benefit. People have to eat to live, and that means animals and plants get raised for human use. Animals shouldn't be mistreated, and when it comes time they should be killed as humanely and painlessly as possible. We have laws to regulate that. And remember, someone put a lot of care into raising these animals to earn a living. Why shouldn't they benefit by selling their stock as products that consumers want?"

QUESTION 3

What moral philosophies does Leslie's father invoke?

Leslie is not satisfied. "How can you say they care for them when they are raising them only to make money? Life is more important than money. If they really cared they'd let them live and be free. At least these carrots didn't have to suffer to be on my plate."

QUESTION 4

What ethical frameworks emerge in Leslie's thinking this time?

Robert replies: "How do you know? You don't know what it's like to be pulled out of the ground and boiled. Anyway, cows don't know anything. They just stand around and chew on grass. They wouldn't even exist except we need them. Human beings are intelligent, they build planes and cities. Animals are only there to serve us. OK, it would be stupid to be cruel to them just for the sake of cruelty, because that wouldn't serve any useful purpose. But if they help us to achieve our lifestyle, we should do it."

QUESTION 5

What more do we learn about Robert's moral thinking here?

Then Leslie's mother, Suzanne, shares her thoughts. "All the same, it does seem that there is useless suffering in the system. Sure, we have laws and regulations, but I am not sure they go far enough. Maybe they look after the interests of humans, but we need to look out for the interests of the animals too.

"I know I would feel much more comfortable eating meat if I knew for sure that animals were genuinely cared for and had the best possible life, and I would even be willing to pay more for meat that came with that assurance."

QUESTION 6

Which of the four ethical frameworks do you detect in Leslie's mother?

Confucian Virtues

But sincerity is not simply a personal attribute, nor merely a means of influencing others. It has political and even metaphysical significance as well.

- "Sincerity means the completion of the self, and the Way [or Tao] is self-directing."
- "Sincerity is the beginning and end of things. Without sincerity there would be nothing. … Sincerity is not only the completion of self, it is that by which all things are completed. The completion of self means humanity. The completion of all things means wisdom. … Therefore whenever [sincerity] is employed, everything done is right."

The cosmic role of sincerity receives powerful statement in another ancient text, the *Great Learning* (or *Adult Education*). This brief text is ascribed to Confucius himself, but ancient commentaries expound its inner meaning.

Sincerity

"There is no greater delight," wrote the Chinese sage Mencius (ca. 371–289 BCE), "than to be conscious of sincerity in self-examination." This nicely demonstrates the great importance that is placed on sincerity, or truthfulness with oneself, in ancient Chinese philosophy.

One early Chinese classic, known as the *Doctrine of the Mean*, emphasizes the role of sincerity in the transformation of self and other (all quotations from *Doctrine of the Mean* and the *Great Learning* are taken or adapted from the work of the prominent scholar of Chinese philosophy Wing-Tsit Chan [1902–1994]).

- "Only those who are absolutely sincere can fully develop their nature. If they can fully develop their nature, they can fully develop the nature of others."
- "Only those who are absolutely sincere can transform others."

- "When things are investigated, knowledge is extended;
  When knowledge is extended, the will becomes sincere;
  When the will is sincere, the mind is rectified;
  When the mind is rectified, the personal life is cultivated;
  When the personal life is cultivated, the family will be regulated;
  When the family is regulated, the state will be in order;
  When the state is in order, there will be peace throughout the world.
  From the Son of Heaven down to the

common people, all must regard cultivation of the personal life as the root and foundation.
There is never a case where the root is in disorder, and yet the branches are in order."

To judge from this, personal, heart-felt *sincerity* is the very fabric from which social order and world peace are woven. A commentary on this text gives sincerity an illuminating definition: it is "allowing no self-deception, as when we hate a bad smell or love a beautiful color." (Wing-Tsit Chan, 1963). Sincerity rests on being honest with ourselves about what we like and dislike. It demands a cultivated sensitivity to states of self, an honesty of feeling. The sincere are "ever watchful over themselves when alone."

From Sincerity to Benevolence

In sincerity one is said to "take one's own feelings as a guide." Applied in our relations with others, sincerity becomes the basis of benevolence, altruism, and respect for others. If you want rank, help others get rank. If you want to turn your merit to your account, help others to do so. Metaphorically, one is applying a measuring square; the result is rectification of the mind:

- "Do not use what you dislike in your superiors in the employment of your inferiors.
  Do not use what you dislike in your inferiors in the service of your superiors.
  Do not use what you dislike in those who are before, to precede those who are behind.
  Do not use what you dislike in those who are behind, to follow those who are before.

Do not use what you dislike on the right, to display toward the left.
Do not use what you dislike on the left, to display toward the right.
This is called applying the principle of the measuring square.'
—Tseng Tzu's commentary on the *Great Learning*

This formulation of the principle of mutual respect (see pp. 62–63) is notable for what it leaves out. It pointedly does *not* presume equality of persons, nor does it prescribe equality of treatment. Above is not the same as below, before need not be treated the same as behind. But in all there is movement from what one dislikes toward appropriate behavior.

Inequality is also presumed in the basic social relationships identified by Confucius. All five of these primary relations require reciprocal mutual respect, but none demand strict equality of treatment or consideration. Regulation of the family depends on three of them (husband–wife, father–son, elder–younger brother), while the other two serve order in the state (prince–minister and mentor–friend). The patriarchal bias in this list rings harsh in modern democratic ears, but the point about reciprocity without equality applies no less to mother–child, elder–younger sister, even to doctor–patient, teacher–student, and employer–employee relationships.

The fundamental respect that runs through all these relationships is humaneness, human-heartedness, a benevolence grounded in our own feelings. Although this virtue applies differently to people depending upon their station in society, it applies to all. For Confucius this virtue of virtues is a largeness of heart that knows no national boundaries and embraces men and women, national and foreigner alike.

DWELLING IN COMPASSION

Compassion is a many-splendored virtue. It has many natures, and can't be contained in any nomenclature. Words like *love, benevolence, mercy, pity, empathy, affection, kindness,* and *care* overlap in significance with the word *compassion*; yet each has its own unique welter of meanings.

No system of contrasting words can suffice to say all that every lovesick heart already knows about compassion, but such systems can help to chart a territory known intuitively to the mapless explorers of the heart. What follows is based on an ancient Buddhist typology of compassions, the doctrine of the Four Limitless Abodes. How many ways can you love all beings?

First, some background theory. An *abode* is an aspect of sublime life. An excellence of mental conduct, it is also an active, constant state in which to dwell during meditation. It is an emotive/intentional orientation to the universe. Each abode has two opposites, *direct* and *indirect*, so that there emerges a kind of state space of these mental realms. Together these interrelated orientations map out a spiritual domain. The *direct opposite* of an abode is an activity oriented in an opposite direction, and so it cannot coexist with the abode in the same mental moment. But each mode also has an *indirect opposite*, which is a lookalike stand-in, a false twin. A sham double and a decoy, it is a mere simulation of the genuine spiritual virtue. The true abodes allow no self-deception. They are limitless in the sense that they are extended universally to all beings. They are dubbed divine on account of their solemnity, and constitute perfections of an enlightened mind.

Soft Compassion

The first limitless abode of compassion is *metta*, or loving-kindness. *Metta* softens the heart, letting goodwill flow outward toward all beings. It is distinguishable from personal affection and from all family or romantic love, which for all its richness is a pale imitation of universal loving-kindness. Affection is the indirect opposite of this compassion. *Metta* is more like the love of all humanity than like the preferential protection for those closest to heart. But all beings, not humanity only, are comprehended in the compassion of *metta*, "even unto the blades of grass." Directly opposite to *metta* is ill-will, malice, or hatred. Hatred lashes out, protecting the illusory boundary around the self. Compassion reaches out, and thereby it weakens that boundary. *Metta* culminates in identification of oneself with all beings. The disarming smile as a gesture represents *metta*.

Trembling Compassion

Karuna is a second limitless abode, also a kind of compassion, the kind that "makes the hearts of the good quiver when others are subject to suffering." Quivering is not softness, so these two are distinct modalities of responsiveness. *Karuna* is the will to remove suffering and reduce harm. Sadness and grief are the inferior namesakes of this harm-reduction approach to compassion; in truth, they are opposed to compassion, and sap its strength. But the mirror image and direct opposite of *karuna* is mean-spirited cruelty, or any deliberate will to harm. As a gesture, this compassion is a comforting embrace.

Overjoyed Compassion

Mudita, or infinite sympathetic joy, a third abode, is yet another form of compassion. If *karuna* removes harms, *mudita* celebrates blessings. This compassion exults in the joys of others, admiring their virtues without taint of envy or selfish desire. As such, it is neither soft nor quivering—so a third quality emerges, another gesture or act of compassion that by no means detracts from the other two. Its gesture is congratulatory, like a warm handshake. Its direct opposite is jealousy, and its ersatz form is stress, agitated excitement, or sympathetic exhilaration.

Composed Compassion

The fourth factor in sublime mentality is not strictly a compassion, but it is food to the other three limitless abodes. It is equanimity, dispassion, the mind in lively balance between desire and aversion.

Equanimity is divinely impartial, embracing pleasure and pain, good and bad, loved and unloved. Its gesture is open arms. Genuine equanimity is a positive state of mind, not a mere absence of habitual reactions. It is an active presence which, if brought in awareness to immediate experience, has consequences in the form of increased sensitivity, enhanced capacity to feel. Equanimity increases subtlety, as one assumes a finer and finer balance. Its cheap imitation is hedonistic indifference, a shoddy knock-off, unintelligent and uncaring.

When equanimity is present, its mirror image opposite cannot be. This antipode is passion, including hatred, jealousy, and tumult. Equanimity is not compassion, but its presence counteracts ill-will, grief, and envy, thus enabling the myriad friendly attitudes of compassion to flourish together.

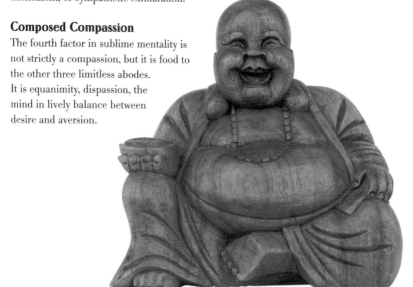

Truth Be Told

THE PROBLEM:

The police are questioning you about the location of a particular person, who is charged with terrible crimes, of which you know him to be completely innocent. If you tell the authorities you have no knowledge of his whereabouts, they will question you further, then leave. However, the person in question is indeed hiding in your home to escape detection. The problem: Should you lie, when lying will prevent a wrongful arrest?

THE METHOD:

People respond to such a challenge in different ways. Some would lie to avoid the wrongful consequences; others would say it is always wrong to lie. The German philosopher Immanuel Kant brought up a case similar to this one, and argued it is your duty always to tell the truth, even if the authorities are suspected of corruption.

Formulate a provisional answer of your own to this question. Next, vary the situational details of the case to see if your answer must change. The case to go on, as presented, is notably lacking in specifics. Such particulars as are given can be treated as variables, and in this way one can examine the durability and applicability of one's ethical intuitions and their principled presumptions.

For example, one relevant variable is the legitimacy of the authorities. If one had a reasonable confidence in the fairness of the judicial processes to which an innocent and wrongly accused individual would be subject, there would be much less fret about handing the person over. If, to the extreme contrary, one had sure knowledge that the authorities were evil and the charges bogus, the risk of harm to the innocent person dramatically escalates. Regarded from this point of view, it would seem that the utility of lying increases with the illegitimacy of the state and its judicial practices.

Another variable is your stowaway. What you know about the person can seem to determine whether it is your duty to lie or a sin. It was simply assumed that you knew this person was innocent of the charges. How had you arrived at that conclusion? Was it trust? Were you with the person when the alleged crimes happened elsewhere? Suppose it were the latter, but that you know this person to be guilty of even worse crimes, of which he is not in the least suspected. Now the principled lie saves a scoundrel's life, yet the truth will send someone to death for a crime they did not commit.

Or again you may have preexisting obligations to the person, such as family ties. While this might not materially change the consequences, there are ethical perspectives from which such prior commitments as these have a weight of their own. Adding loyalty to the reasons to lie make it that much more tempting. Indeed, the problem becomes interesting in another way if it is assumed that the family member in hiding is guilty. Then the dilemma transforms into a conflict between duty to family and duty to the state (or society, or humanity as a whole).

A third factor is the nature of the crimes, which were left unspecified. They might be against property or against persons. Suppose theft is the crime, terrible for its scale, but that the real perpetrator is a regular Robin Hood, stealing the ill-gotten wealth of the rich and redistributing it to the exploited poor. The fugitive under your bed is innocent, but if captured might reveal where Robin Hood is hiding. Now a lie protects the innocent and shields a crime, albeit a heroic one. But when violent crimes are involved, public passions are roused. Suppose an angry mob arrives behind the authorities, threatening to rampage unless your guest is delivered to them. Here lying to save an innocent could provoke a riot.

THE SOLUTION:

So far we have looked mostly at consequences, as if the ethical dilemmas had always to be resolved by an examination of the states of affairs they bring about. This consequentialist presumption is disputed by deontologists or rights-based theorists. But in this alternate camp too there is division, for there are different points of view within the non-consequentialist tradition of ethics.

According to deontologists, lying is always wrong. But some consider it your duty never to lie, others that the evil of lying is sometimes necessary, not, indeed, for the sake of worldly outcomes, but rather for the sake of a principle higher than truthfulness, like sanctity of life. The latter view might seem like consequentialism all over again, but violation of moral principle is not technically a consequence (since it is not utility). It may be your duty to lie, even if it is always wrong to lie, because your duty might occasionally include ethically necessary evils.

3

Metaphysics and Spirituality

Metaphysics is the home of philosophy's biggest

questions. Why are we here? Where are we anyway?

What sort of world is this? Who and what am I?

What is freedom and liberation? And is the mind

just the brain? We dip into these problems as into

bottomless pools, and explore world-forming

concepts such as cause, substance, being, space,

time, identity, self, god, and karma. But is there any

reality to any of these concepts? Or are they all

mere appearance?

APPEARANCE AND REALITY

An Indian Illusion

You are making your way in the dark, barely able to see the ground a few steps ahead of you. Suddenly you are startled by a snake coiled in the path. Before you can react, you see it is only a rope left lying in the path.

In the event, you perceived the rope as a snake, before you saw it to be what it really was. Your engagement with your reality involves much emotion and semantic memory, but these shifted radically toward the positive when the illusion departed. The rope did not cause the illusion, nor did it suffer change by appearing and then not appearing to be a snake. The rope did not change, did not even appear to change. But the appearance it presented did change. The appearance of snake really happened, but the reality of snake only appeared.

The Snake Is Your Experience

This tale was told as a metaphysical instruction by Sankara, the great non-dualist and exponent of *Advaita Vedanta*. Just as you superimposed a snake upon that rope, ascribing to it qualities that do not properly belong to it, so is it that you perceive your reality.

True reality is not changed by its changing appearances. Granted, it appears to change, but only the appearance is changing. True reality is not in fact different from your experience, although it does appear that way to you. Truth is not the author or the creator or cause of your superimposition; for that you must accept responsibility yourself. But in your own nature, you are not different from Truth. It only appears that way. You are the rope.

Substance Is What's Real (or Really Real)

Nobody likes anyone who's all for show. Philosophically, what has "substance" is that which is ultimate, not reducible to anything else, whatever has its own independent reality. Sometimes this independence is relative, rather than absolute, so that everyday objects that come together and fall apart have— while they last—a relative independence. However, some views, like Sankara's non-dualism, institute an ultimate truth beyond the fallacy of everyday experience. There is real, then there is really real.

If substance is what is ultimately real, the next question is: What is its essential nature? Essence is *whatness*, substance is *thatness*. A metaphysics may claim or aim to grasp the essence, define the substance, and give an account of what ultimately is. Or it may denounce the attempt, not on wholly skeptical grounds (for skeptics abandon metaphysics), but on account of flaws in the very notion of essence. Essentialism is its own metaphysics, but it is not the only metaphysics.

What Are Your Ontological Commitments?

Your ontological commitments are the things that you believe exist, items the reality of which you are prepared to accept. If you believe in the tooth fairy, she is among your ontological commitments. If you believe there is a God or that you have an eternal soul, you are committed to their existence, so they are in your ontology. You may be unwilling to doubt the reality of material objects, even atoms you have never seen and quasars you have barely

heard of. If so, then they are all among your ontological commitments. You can farm out your ontology to the experts, such as scientists or theologians, who will gladly perform this metaphysical labor on your behalf, or you can try to think for yourself about what really is.

What Are My Ontological Commitments?

- **Is there a God? What's God like?**
- **Is time physical or subjective?**
- **Is mind distinct from matter?**
- **Does matter have ultimate constituents?**
- **Is causation a force or merely a regularity?**
- **Who am I? What am I? Am I free?**
- **Will I exist after my death?**
- **Is there a predetermined purpose to the universe, to life, to human existence, to my existence?**
- **Do infinities exist?**

STYLES OF METAPHYSICAL SUBSTANCE

For ancient atomists such as Democritus, atoms alone are substantial; everything else is but a temporary agglomeration of atoms. Plato regarded the timeless *Forms* or *Ideas* as substantial, while everyday objects are less real shadows or images of them. For Aristotle, everyday objects are substantial forms, not mere imitations nor reducible to the interaction of atoms.

Descartes is called a substance dualist for his belief in the independent existence of mind and body. (His so-called mind–body problem is to determine how and where these two substantially different realities interact.) Spinoza replied that there was but one absolutely infinite substance: God or Nature. Hume's skeptical doubts called into question all knowledge of substantial (that is, real or ultimate) causation.

PYTHAGORAS

As mentioned earlier, the first Greek philosophers were physicalist metaphysicians, since they took the source and substance of the world to be a material principle, like water or fire. The development of geometry pulled philosophy in a new direction, with its lure of a rational and deductive system. In geometry, truth is not accidental. Mathematical philosophies arose.

The Real as Rational

Prominent among this second wave was a semi-legendary figure named Pythagoras. To Pythagoras is attributed the remarkable view that all is number, or ratios of numbers. Consider a string, like a guitar string, stretched tight so that it makes a particular note—for simplicity, say middle C. If one presses the string down at the half-way point (the 12th fret on a guitar), the resulting note will be one octave higher.

In hearing the octave, Pythagoras asserted, one hears the ratio of 1:2. Other intervals (notes) are obtained by dividing the string at different points, using other ratios. By pressing down one-third of the way along the length (in effect, the 7th fret on the guitar), one hears the 3:2 ratio (also called the perfect fifth, in this case G above middle C). The point for Pythagoras was that we hear the ratio itself in the music.

Turning his attention to the cosmos, and inheriting centuries of speculations from his extensive travels, Pythagoras also found regular ratios among the orbiting planets. The movement of the planets and the sun was a "music of the spheres," a heavenly harmony accessible to the mathematically literate. *If you would know the world, learn mathematics.* That is the lesson of Pythagoras, and it rings true today across the mathematical sciences.

The Surd and the Absurd

Pythagoras is most famous for his discovery of the geometrical theorem that bears his name. The Pythagorean Theorem, though celebrated, also exploded the Pythagorean philosophy that the real is rational (all is ratio). To see how, it helps to think about numbers geometrically. As in musical harmony, ratios and numbers are to be thought of as concrete and spatial.

Consider any right triangle, with sides of lengths a, b, and c. Construct a square outside the triangle based on the length of each side of the triangle, shown above right. Then, the Pythagorean Theorem can be conveniently expressed as follows:

$$a^2 + b^2 = c^2$$

In other words, the square of the hypotenuse of a right-angled triangle is equal to the sum of the squares of the two

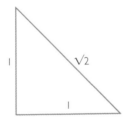

sides. Geometrically, it means that the area of rectangle C is equal to the combined areas of rectangles A and B.

The problem arises already from the simplest case of this theorem, the unit triangle, which is to say a right triangle where a=b=1 (a unit may be any distance: an inch or a mile). Given the above formula, and some simple calculations, we can determine the length of the hypotenuse c as follows:

$$1^2 + 1^2 = c^2$$

$$1 + 1 = 2 = c^2$$

Taking the square root of both sides, we have:

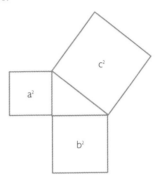

$$c = \sqrt{2} = 1.4142135623730950$$

$$488016887242097 \ldots$$

The square root of 2 is only partially given here, because its decimal expansion is infinite and non-repeating. (If it were finite or repeating, it could be expressed as a ratio.) This means that c is a *surd*, a geometrical quantity corresponding to what are now called *irrational numbers*. Despite not being expressible as a ratio of units, the hypotenuse c is no less real than the sides a and b. In effect, Pythagoras was the first to learn that there were real numbers other than the rational numbers (i.e., fractions) alone. Even today, the set containing both the rational and the irrational numbers is known as the set of *real* numbers, and forms the mathematical basis of the space–time continuum (see Space, pp. 96–97).

Aristotle's Metaphysics

> "All men by nature desire to know."
>
> —*Aristotle*

Aristotle's World

The earth was at the center of Aristotle's cosmos. The moon and the stars and the wandering planets (including the sun) moved in fixed concentric spheres around the earth, which occupied the lowest place. He saw something eternal, hence divine, in the perfectly circular orbits traced by those heavenly bodies of fire, which were located above us, not merely far away. As earth belongs at the lowest place, fire belongs at the highest. Aristotle also held that we participated in this divinity after our death, not indeed as individuals, but in virtue of our form or kind, our *rationality*.

Below the moon of Aristotle's universe, motion always has a beginning and an end. This disappointing law has sunk into anyone who has tried to throw a ball so far it will never land, or so high it will never come down (like fire). Limits and death are facts of the sublunary world. But nature always acts on purpose, he fundamentally believed, and so the motions and activities of plants and animals—including rational animals such as ourselves—must be *for* something, must have some purpose, must exist in order to fulfill some positive function. Aristotle's metaphysics is

teleological (from the Greek *telos*, meaning end or purpose, function or natural work). The *telos* is that for the sake of which something exists or is undertaken. It is one of the four Aristotelian causes (see opposite).

The Essence of Things (or: Substantial Forms)

On earth, some things are manmade or artificial, others exist by nature. Both are *substantial* in the metaphysical sense (that is, *ultimately real*), making a science of them possible (contrary to Plato, for whom the Forms by themselves were substantial).

Just as we make artifacts like buildings or tools to serve some purpose, so too natural objects, in Aristotle's view, come into being for the sake of some natural end. Tools don't do anything; we do things with tools. What distinguishes natural substances, in Aristotle's view, is the *source of natural motion* they carry within themselves. They possess an *internal principle* of motion and rest. Stones by nature move downward, fire goes up. Plants throw roots down and grow, each after its own kind. Each species of animal has its own form of growth and locomotion, plus various instinctual (hence natural) forms of activity. Plants take nutrition through their roots, animals through their mouths. Both reproduce, which Aristotle likens to a consolation prize for not being able to live eternally. Throughout nature, Aristotle concluded, the lower exists for the sake of the higher.

The Causes of Things

Concerning the nature or *essence* of natural and artificial substances, it seemed to Aristotle obvious that *what something* is cannot be the same as *what something is made of*. The statue of Socrates is not simply marble, but marble in the *form* of Socrates. The form of Socrates is what makes that marble a statue of Socrates. A heap of table parts is not a table, but those same parts duly arranged constitute the table. Here geometrical arrangement is the form or essence of the table, not the material it is made out of. That form or arrangement allows the pieces to serve the purpose of a table.

In these examples, form determines function (*telos*). So too, thought Aristotle, throughout the world of nature. The arrangement of the parts of plants and animals allows for those beings to be made up of organs (a word that means *functional part*), and these serve the various purposes of life, such as nutrition, reproduction, sensation, or locomotion. The eye is made to see with; that is its purpose or function. The virtue of the eye is its functioning well, its seeing clearly (see Virtue; pp. 62–63).

All told, Aristotle recognized four factors of explanation— these are known as the four causes, which are all required in any complete account of natural change, growth, and decay.

1. **Material cause**—the stuff out of which something is made.
2. **Formal cause**—the form (shape, arrangement, or functional organization).
3. **Moving cause**—the action or process that brings the object or change about.
4. **Final cause**—that *for the sake of which* something exists or changes (*telos* or end).

By nature, the formal cause is primary. Form determines function (*telos*), but it is also the source of natural motion within. It is the beginning and end of change. The primacy of form in Aristotle reveals the influence of Plato, and even the Socratic legacy (see Plato, pp. 20–21). But whereas Plato located the Forms in a realm apart from matter, Aristotle embeds form *within matter*, inseparable from it.

Psyche as Form

For Aristotle, the *psyche* or soul is the *form* of the living being, thus also its internal source of motion and its final cause, the purpose of its being, its *sake*. The human soul is rationality; of all forms, it alone can exist separately, and so at death we join the eternal rationality of the heavenly spheres.

CAUSAL POWERS

Plato: Cause as Essence

For Plato, the true cause of things being what they are is their archetype or template, their *eidos* or ideal essence. Things are what they are through participating in a shared form or nature, which Plato conceived of as existing separate and apart from the ephemeral material realm disclosed to us by our senses. Thus, the form of justice, intelligible only to the intellect, is the same, whether in the city or in the psyche. It is a harmonious three-part functioning of either (see pp. 104–105).

Aristotle: Causation as Actualization

Aristotle retained the Socratic notion of an ideal essence, but embedded it in matter and flanked it with other sorts of causal explanations—other "whys." Preeminent among these, the *eidos*, or "formal" cause is responsible for making things what they are; that is, it specifies what kind of thing it is. Whether an ax or an eye, the form is the arrangement of parts that allows for appropriate functioning, chopping, or seeing. The form of the ax exists first potentially in the mind of the toolmaker, then actually in the finished tool, then in an even higher grade of actuality in the use of the tool. Likewise, the form of the eye allows it to see, but its highest-grade actuality lies in the use of the eye to see (i.e., in actually seeing).

The psyche, too, is the actual living of a body. The highest-grade actuality of the human soul is an actual life, a living individual. For Aristotle, there is no individual survival after death, only a sort of eternity in kind. We partake in divine reason; the world is fundamentally intelligible.

Aristotle's explanatory style presumes that all nature works for a purpose. A world with final causes built in is a world imbued with value, an "enchanted world." Modern science disenchanted nature by striking final causes, and all teleology, from the approved list of scientific explanations.

Galileo: The Colorless Machine

A principle of explanatory parsimony, Occam's Razor states that one should not multiply entities without necessity. Do not saddle your explanations or ontologies with extraneous complexity. Named for William of Occam (ca. 1280–1349), it is applied to Plato's tangled beard to excavate forms, essences, and final causes from the realm of metaphysics.

Early modern science continued to trim hairy metaphysics, preferring epistemological thrift and explanatory economy. Galileo (1564–1642) totally rejected final causes from science. God may have his purposes with the world, but our science is not to reason why. Mechanical, measurable, and demonstrable regularities were the laws of his world.

Galileo warned that we read purposes into things, much as we read colors into them. The colors that appear in objects are not in the objects. They result in consciousness from the interaction of light, the surfaces of objects, and the physiology of the eye and brain. Red light is not red in its nature. In today's terms, it is a certain frequency of wave that is able to produce a red experience in us. Color is in

consciousness, or in the brain–world
relationship, not in the object itself.
Purposes, too, we project onto nature.

Physical Necessity
and Natural Law

Logical necessity is independent of
circumstance. Marriage does not bestow
a bachelor with a spouse; it ends
bachelorhood and creates a husband.
The circumstances have changed, but all
bachelors remain unwed. Even the duties
of marriage do not change; what changes
is that they are now incumbent on two
more people.

Physical necessity is at once more
substantial than logical necessity and more
compelling than an ethical ideal. A mere
lapse of judgment can ruin a marriage; it
takes a miracle to ruin a physical necessity.

Gravity compels so thoroughly that
even "defying gravity" is a misnomer.
Pumice is a rock that floats: expectation,
not gravity, is contradicted. The bumblebee
may defy mathematical physicists, but not
physical necessity. The so-called anti-
gravity reflexes that make it look so easy
to Fred Astaire may be a marvel, but they
are not a miracle. Zero-gravity is far from
inconsistent with gravity—it occurs
predictably according to gravitational laws.

Mechanical cause is sometimes
described as explanation by "pushes and
pulls," symbolized by the springs or
enmeshing cogs on interlocking gears.
Billiards is the canonical metaphor (see
Hume, pp. 44–45). But the image of a key
turning a lock is a useful contrast. Ask
Hume's question about perception of
causation about your experience of opening
a lock with a key that fits. Do you have a
sensory impression of the physical necessity?

KARMA AS CAUSE

The word *karma* has a root meaning
action, by extension, *cause*. Emphasis is
often put on its meaning as effect (as
when we ascribe present fortune or
misfortune to karma). This latter usage,
though popular, is arguably an instance
of the confirmation bias. It can also
amount to blaming the victim.

Rather than regarding karma as a
non-material moral residue of past
deeds, a cosmic comeuppance, or fate,
you can think of it as mental volitions,
predispositions to act grounded in
mental habit. Karma in the moment is
mental habit patterns, the cause of so
many of our thoughts, words, and
deeds, generally clouded by ignorance
based in self. Transcending karma is
merely overcoming habit-patterns,
freedom-enhancing self-knowledge,
and self-mastery. Karma in its broad
definition does not even presuppose
reincarnation.

MODALITIES: WAYS OF BEING (TRUE)

Necessity and Possibility

Some propositions are true, others are false. But some truths are *necessarily* true, and some falsehoods *necessarily* false. A (logically) necessary truth is a proposition that by its very nature has to be true; it could not possibly have been false. No bachelor will ever have a spouse (although many will become husbands and cease to be bachelors). Seven and six can't help being thirteen. Necessary truths are true no matter what. Other propositions depend for their truth on various conditions that may or may not obtain.

A proposition that is necessarily false is one that asserts the logically impossible, an overt absurdity like 0=1, *squares are round, green is red*, or 6+7≠13. A logical falsehood is not just something extremely unlikely, like *man bites dog* or *rocks float on water*. It has to be intrinsically impossible.

There is a third class, called *contingent* propositions, which are neither necessarily true nor necessarily false. Contingent propositions may happen to be true, but they are not bound to be. They may also happen to be false, though they are not absurd or impossible. Things just may not turn out that way. Contingent propositions depend on circumstances. You could turn right, but you turn left instead. The earth might have had two moons, but in fact it has just one. Not every truth had to be the way it is. (For examples of contingent propositions, see the sections on conditionals [p. 138–139] and quantifiers [p. 142–143].)

Diamonds and Boxes

We can capture these ideas in simple symbols:

◊P stands for "It is possible that P" or "P is possible."

[]P stands for "It is necessary that P" or "P is necessary."

A necessary falsehood can now be symbolized in either of two ways. Let ¬P stand for the negation of P ("It is not the case that P" or "not P"). Then:

¬◊P
"It is not possible that P is the case" or "P is not possible."

[]¬P
"It is necessary that P is not the case" or "P is necessarily not the case."

Contingency is more complex than mere possibility. It can also be expressed in two equivalent ways:

◊P & ¬[]P
"P is possible, but not necessary."

◊P & ◊¬P
"P is possible, but not-P is also possible."

Notice that there is a big difference between ¬[]P and []¬P, between "It ain't necessarily so" and "It necessarily ain't so." Notice too: if P is contingent, so is ¬P.

Possible Worlds

The *actual world* (not the earth, but all time and the universe) is the sum of all truths, contingent or necessary. It is a maximally consistent "set," since the addition of any other proposition to it would render it logically inconsistent. (See why? If a proposition is not in the set originally, it is false, and its negation is already in.)

A *possible world* is any maximally consistent sum of propositions. Since it is logically consistent, it will not contain any necessary falsehoods (which are inconsistent all on their own). Since it is maximal, it will include all necessary truths. A possible world is a total way the world could be. There are many possible worlds. Possible worlds talk allows us to elucidate modal concepts. We can say that []P is true if P is true in every possible world. In other words, P would have been true no matter how the world turned out.

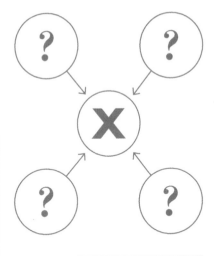

EXERCISES

Our two symbols are *redundant*: either can be defined in terms of the other.

1. Using only P, ¬, and ◊, find an expression that means the same thing as []P.

2. Using only P, ¬, and [], find an expression that means the same thing as ◊P.

SPACE: FRONTIER WITHOUT FINALITY

Geometry by Numbers

Perhaps you are familiar with the Cartesian plane, the intersecting x–y axes of school mathematics. Named after its inventor, Descartes, it gives a way to identify any point in a two-dimensional plane by an ordered pair of real numbers, $\langle x,y \rangle$. It is readily extended to 3D, so that any point in space can be represented by an ordered triple, $\langle x,y,z \rangle$.

Descartes tells us he hit upon the idea of representing points in space with a coordinate number system while philosophizing late one morning in bed. He observed a fly zipping about his room, and realized that, if he labeled one corner of his room as the origin, $\langle 0,0,0 \rangle$, he could specify every point in the path of the bug's flight with three real numbers. One might write the fly's location as a function of time: $f(t) = \langle a,b,c \rangle$—*at time t, the insect's position has coordinates x=a, y=b, and z=c.*

It became possible to express geometrical problems as problems about mathematical functions of numbers, which led to powerful new methods of solving many physical and geometrical problems.

Matter as the Extended Substance

Thinking of geometry through real-number arithmetic has a special significance for Descartes' metaphysics, since he considered matter in its very essence to be *extension*. And geometry is the science of extension. In effect, the material world operates on mathematical (indeed, *mechanical*) principles. The laws of nature are written in the language of mathematics.

Descartes grasped the essential nature of matter before he was sure it actually existed, before even his proof of God's existence. To be extended is simply to take up space. All matter takes up space, and all space is taken up (Descartes, like Aristotle, rejected the possibility of a vacuum). For Descartes, as for Plato, the *intellect* directly perceives the essence, which is not known through the senses. All the sensory properties of wax change if it is melted, but the extension is there unless and until the wax is destroyed.

If the essence of matter is extension, a science of nature should dispense with all teleological explanations. The physical world of which Descartes was certain (after all his doubt) is a mechanical world, shorn of a natural purpose or final cause. It is the modern world.

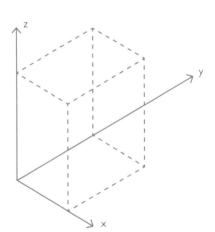

Is the World Finite or Infinite?

Does outer space extend forever or only for a finite stretch?

Suppose you were to find yourself at the very edge of the world, beyond which lies nothing at all, not even empty space. Standing at the uttermost limit of space, you might wonder whether it is possible for you to extend your arm into that beyond. If nothing is there, there is nothing to stop you. But if there is no space there, there is no place there to receive your arm, and you will find it impenetrable. Nothingness should appear solid.

In ancient times, the heavenly vault of "fixed stars" was observed to rotate every day about the North Star, the "pole star." So the finitude of the world seemed obvious. Now we know the illusion arises from the rotation of the earth, which is not immediately perceptible to us. The stars are not fixed but many different distances away from us, and moving further away ever faster.

The World Kant Saw in the Mirror

For Kant, space does not represent things *as they are in themselves*, but only things *as they appear to us*. Things in themselves have no spatial properties. Geometrical truths get their necessity from the way things *have to appear* to us. Space is a form of intuition, of our capacity to receive immediate sensible representations of things external to us and to each other. Space is the *a priori* form of outer intuition.

One may crudely compare Kant's view of the mind to the curves and wrinkles on the surface of a circus mirror. Light falling on the mirror may be ordered in itself, but to be reflected in this mirror it must be ordered by the form

IS THE WORLD FINITE BUT UNBOUNDED?

Suppose that every physical body in the universe were simultaneously dilated, everything expanded in the same proportion. Despite this remarkable change, would we in fact be able to detect it? All our measuring sticks would also have grown, so none of our measurements would differ from what it was before.

of the surface. The mind's receptivity actively imposes a determinate order on our immediate experience.

Kant asked doubters to compare their own right hand with its mirror image (now using a standard mirror). The reflection will be a left hand, but otherwise identical to the original. The two are completely equal and similar, and have identical internal spatial relationships, yet they are not congruent and cannot be substituted for each other. The difference, which spatial intuition reveals immediately, is wholly unintelligible to thought. What makes the right hand right is the rest of space into which it fits.

FREEDOM AND NECESSITY

Choice Is an Event

If every event is caused, then all your free choices are caused. But to be caused is to be necessitated. So all your free choices are necessitated. Either freedom is necessitated, or there is no freedom.

At issue here is metaphysical freedom, not political liberty or moral autonomy. For your choice to be free, it must be the case that you could have done otherwise. But if choice is necessitated, it could not have been otherwise. What is necessitated had to happen, and so your choice had to happen. Either that or it is an uncaused event. But no event can be uncaused.

In this metaphysical circle, many a philosophical dog has chased its tail to death.

Questioning Determinism

Underlying this reasoning is the major determinist assumption that *every event is caused, hence necessitated*. Events do not occur out of the blue. That is, we may not *expect* them, we may be surprised by them, but then some unknown factors or conditions must have brought them about. If there is no sufficient cause for an event, it is not clear why it should ever have happened, since its not happening is also an event without a cause. An event can't both happen and not happen. [](E or ¬E)

Our metaphysical confidence is not attended by epistemic success. That is, we don't always know what the cause is, or fully understand all the conditions that bring an event about. We have more confidence that there always are causes, than that we can always find them. This curious obstinacy is the blithe optimism of science, convinced that the truth is out there, even if it should endlessly evade our search.

Questioning Causation

It is one thing to endorse science in principle, and share its confidence in causal explanation. It is another to cast suspicion on our psychological experience of causation. However, the two come together nicely in scientific investigation into our *perception* of causation.

Hume claimed the sensory impression of causation to be absent, not to be found in experience even if carefully examined. "All events seem loose and separate. One event follows another; but we never can observe any tie between them. They seem *conjoined*, but never *connected*" (Hume, *Enquiry*, Sc. VII Pt II). Hume assumes we can have no knowledge of causation if we cannot locate such an impression. Many thinkers have inspected for themselves and found none. What do you find?

The Belgian psychologist Albert Michotte believed he had experimentally isolated just such an impression of mechanical causation. His famous launching effect is the main illustration. It can be demonstrated with many devices, perhaps the simplest being shadows on a screen. Essentially, Michotte was easily able to create the illusory perception of causation by moving the shadows in certain paths in relations to each other.

One shadow moves at a steady rate until it appears to contact another, which until then was still but at once begins to move in the same direction and rate as the first one, which now lags behind. The one appears to strike the other and to set it in motion. Slight variations (such as a brief interval before the second shadow begins to move) destroy the perceptual effect entirely. Similar casual illusions are everywhere in animation today.

Michotte's experimental results led him to the view that we perceive events and actions, including causal events, not mere objects in motion. We perceive things doing things to other things.

This refutation of Hume has a price: We do have an impression of causation, but it is susceptible to illusion—we see causation even when it is not there.

Questioning Freedom

If perception of causation is, or at least can be, an illusion, then our perception of our own causal doings is, or at least can be, an illusion.

Perhaps you have had the experience of changing the TV channel with a remote control, when a room light suddenly goes on. By chance, someone else has flipped the switch at the very moment you pressed the button on the remote. If the timing is just right, it can feel like you did it. One can experience the distinct impression of having caused the light to go on.

What do you think? Is your own causation of your actions a perceptual illusion? Throughout your day, interrupt your regular activities to ask: "Am I choosing this action? What is the cause of my behavior?"

EXERCISES

Watch some people playing billiards, and examine the contact of one ball upon another and the resulting motion. Do you get a sensory impression of causal action?

THIS IS NOT A BIKE

Taking the question of identity personally

**Whoever you are, you are not finished.
Who you are is a journey.**

By Bike

Michael and Ian were like chalk and cheese—Michael was a perfectionist and Ian an inveterate hoarder. Take Michael's bicycle. Whenever any part of it became even slightly worn, Michael would replace it, and all the discarded parts ended up in Ian's workshop. Before long, every part was replaced, and Ian was eventually able to reassemble the old parts and reconstitute the original bicycle. He and Michael went cycling together, and the strange thing is that each of them thought he was riding Mike's bike! Who was right?

By Ship

The problem with Mike's bikes is identical to the ancient problem about the Ship of Theseus (except that some of the parts have been changed). Theseus' victory over the minotaur in the labyrinth of Crete was commemorated every seven years using this ship. Over time the planks and other parts had to be replaced. Eventually, entirely new materials composed the ship. Was it the same ship?

There is no question that it was the only ship entitled to participate in the ceremony. So perhaps the identity of the ship is a *social* ascription. Is your identity a social construct?

Cell by Cell

It is sometimes said that the body totally regenerates itself every seven years. Although this is an urban myth, recent research estimates average cell age to be seven to ten years. Still, cells of many types are continuously replaced, and much of the body is rebuilt over time. By the age of 65, you will have gone through six skeletons, four sets of muscles and guts, and probably over 30 livers. Your red blood cells will have been renewed almost 200 times. Your external skin will only be a couple weeks old, perhaps your 1700th epidermis. Only the lens inside your eye will be as old as you, perhaps your heart muscle cells, and probably the neurons of your cerebral cortex. (Wade, 2005; Spalding et al., 2005.)

If your personal identity is a product of your brain, at least it has a relatively stable physical basis. Stability is relative. Collapse is inevitable. Will you still be around after you die? Will you be there at your funeral, able bodilessly to witness your own corpse or ashes? Or are you only your living body?

By Memory

For English philosopher John Locke (1632–1704), the fact that you remember having experiences is sufficient to show you are the same person now as then. Conscious memory is the glue of self, since it is the effective criterion of being the same person.

Questions about the identity of *persons* are therefore totally different from questions about identity of *substance*, like the sameness of bikes, boats, or bodies. Accessible memory is the criterion of sameness of persons, not continuity of substance.

Even continuity of *spiritual* substance is irrelevant to personal identity, says Locke. Suppose the same soul is born in different bodies, in different lifetimes. If the later one cannot consciously remember the first, then this soul has two persons, as well as two bodies. Contrariwise, Locke claims (with some hesitation due to obscurity), two immaterial or spiritual substances would be the same person if they shared the same conscious memories.

BY GOLLY

So who are you really? Are you your body? Are you the organized activity of your brain cells? Are you a socially constructed and ascribed identity? Is your existence dependent on ritual recognition?

Or is your consciousness enough to unite you? Have you lost those parts of yourself you have forgotten? Would amnesia destroy you?

Or do you require an immaterial substance to tide you over from this life to the next, or to cover your lapses in memory of your past lives?

Locke argues for his view by inviting the following fantasy. Suppose in an accident your little finger is cut off. Your consciousness continues as usual, only in the removed finger, not in the rest of the body. You remember having been attached to that body, not that finger having been attached to you. In the accident, a new and separate consciousness, cut off from your memories, arises in the remaining body. Would it not be unjust—asks Locke—for *it* to enjoy the rewards of your past actions (like your paycheck)? Would it not be equally wrong to punish you, the finger, for the misdeed of the body's new occupant?

Even God, Locke suggests, will only punish you at Judgment Day for sins you can be made to remember.

THE PROBLEM:

Imagine you have a transporter that can scan your body through and through, store all the information regarding its configuration that is relevant to you being you, and then transmit that information to any desired location, where a receiving device will process it and, using organic materials on hand, construct a complete and exact duplicate of your brain and body, down to the last molecule. The entire process takes a few seconds, and leaves no psychological mark. You arrive at your destination with all your thoughts, feelings, beliefs, and memories intact. The space-machine is 100% safe and effective. The question is: Would you go? And if you arrived, would it still be you?

THE METHOD:

This problem is based on Derek Parfit's *Teletransporter* thought experiment, which was presented in 1984 and has been discussed by philosophers extensively in the decades since. It is constructed so as to reveal underlying philosophical assumptions whichever side your intuitions first lead you. Parfit thinks it shows the unimportance of personal identity.

It is important to recognize that this transporter will not give you a better body, so you ought not be tempted here by the fruits of a different thought experiment. By the same token, you will not end up with a worse body, for we get to assume

that there are never malfunctions in the technology. Don't let the risk of travel accident dissuade you from using the transporter. At your destination, you will find your body has been rebuilt exactly as you are now, as robust or as frail, with every perfection and blemish, you now (however knowingly) possess.

One key assumption is that the replication process preserves psychological continuity and connectedness. To the extent that your psychological attributes are determined by your brain and body, these are replicated too. Experientially, teletransportation is similar to a long blink; you close your eyes for some time and open them in another location—or rather, someone opens them in the new place who has your exact psychological history. The question is: Are you that someone?

THE SOLUTION:

There is no solution to this sort of puzzle. Practical solutions are out of the question when problems are by hypothesis impossible. The point is not to find the correct answer but to explore our reactions and the underlying assumptions they commit us too. If you feel no existential threat at your current body being obliterated, since a duplicate is guaranteed at your destination, it may be because you don't think you are your body. If a felt continuity, despite a material discontinuity, is enough to preserve your identity through teletransportation, you apparently don't believe a persistent soul or continuous spiritual substance is necessary for you to remain who you are.

You can push the self-exploration further by considering variations of the original case. Unlike above, these variations are not intended as reasons to decide one way or another about the original case. Instead, they are independent thought experiments serving the same self-exploratory purpose, pointing out underlying philosophical assumptions that may be operative when you decide you would, or you would never, step into the transporter.

- Suppose your body is not destroyed in the process, but a replica is generated remotely. There are now two qualitatively identical but numerically distinct candidates to be yourself. Are you still your replica? How can you be identical to the replica when your body is destroyed, but distinct from it if your original body survives intact?

- Taking this variation further, suppose that both you and the replica have equal degrees of psychological continuity and connectedness with your past self. Has your replica equal right to your inheritance as you? Does your physical continuity give you any privileged status vis-à-vis your doppelgänger? Can it really matter so much which particular carbon atoms you are made of?

- Once again your body survives the scanning, but is slightly injured, reducing your psychological continuity and connectedness with your past self to below that of your replica. You are less connected to your past self than your replica, but are you less you than your replica?

- You have been sentenced to a terrible, laborious fate on a remote planet, a life term from which you can escape only if you are replicated, in which case there is a 50–50 chance that your replica will be sent in your place. Does it matter to you whether you or your replica goes? If you were prepared originally to teletransport yourself, but now prefer your replicate to be sent in your place, are you not condemning yourself anyway?

- Suppose one hemisphere of your brain dies. You survive and retain a high degree of psychological continuity and connectedness with your past self. Still you, right? Now suppose your right and left brain are surgically separated and both halves survive, each maintaining psychological continuity and connectedness. Can they both be you?

THE CONFLICTS WITHIN PLATO'S SOUL

How many parts do you have on your mental insides? When you look within, do you find divisions? Boundaries? What about oppositions? Plato used an argument from opposite action to argue that the human psyche or soul had three parts with independent, and sometimes opposing, functions. One can compare Plato's theory to Freud's more familiar division of the soul into id, ego, and superego, but the parts are different and have different functions.

Plato's Three-Part Psyche

We know with one part, are angry with another, and lust with a third. Suppose you are very thirsty but the only water is salt water. You know enough not to drink it—it will only further dehydrate you and make you thirstier. So you refrain out of good sense. Here Plato finds the appetite (a part of the soul that experiences desires) in opposition to reason, which forbids drinking and overpowers the desire.

Now suppose you come upon the scene of a horrible accident. Authorities are in attendance, so they merely wave you past. As you drive by, you wonder if you should glance at the carnage. Part of you wants to, but another part is disgusted by your own interest and resists. In such a struggle Plato detected three factors: *reason* condemns the *desire* to look, and *anger* at oneself builds up. He imagines a similar case where a man gave in to his desire to look at dead bodies, while yet regarding the desire as repugnant and beneath him. The self-anger he experienced is in alliance with the judgment of his reason.

Elsewhere Plato finds reason chiding anger, so they can't be functions of the same part. In any case, children and animals can be angry before they can reason. So, all three parts must be distinct.

A Symphony of Virtue

Although these are parts of the human *psyche* or soul, Plato associates them with locations in the body. Reason is situated in the head, anger in the breast, and the appetites are in the belly and loins. Proper regulation of these psychological functions meant that the head should rule the heart and the passions. Reason over passion—this was wise rulership of the soul, which kept the other parts in check, establishing a three-part psychic harmony that Plato saw as the very Form (*eidos*) of justice.

Note that excellent functioning of each part of the soul is a virtue: Wisdom is the excellence of reason, courage the excellence of the spirited part that feels anger, and moderation is the best course for the appetites. Justice is the well-functioning whole.

These are the famous cardinal virtues (see Virtue, pp. 62–63). The three-part form of justice is also discernible at the level of the city-state, in the harmonious social order of Plato's utopian caste system.

In a memorable image, Plato compares the appetites to a many-headed beast, with "a ring of heads of tame and wild beasts," ever-changing and always growing new ones. The spirited part that feels anger in the heart is likened to a lion (although elsewhere to a guard dog, loyal, sniffing out friend and foe, capable of true opinion but not genuine knowledge). The reasoning faculty of the soul has human form, but also something divine about it. This multiform monster is the human soul. The just soul is a well-managed menagerie.

Eternal Injustice?

Plato firmly believed in the immortality of the soul, but only of the reasoning part. The other parts were incapable of knowledge and too closely associated to the body to be divine. Anyway, nothing eternal could have parts or be composite (because anything with parts must eventually fall apart).

A consequence of this, it would seem, is that the eternal soul cannot be a just soul (it is not a three-part harmony).

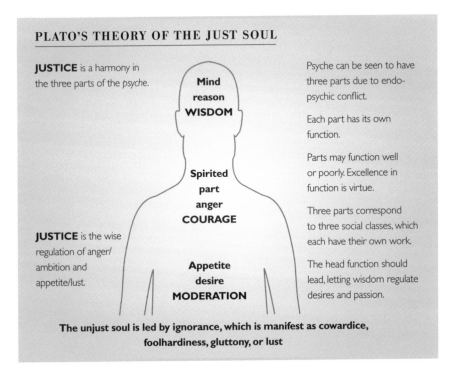

PLATO'S THEORY OF THE JUST SOUL

JUSTICE is a harmony in the three parts of the *psyche*.

Mind
reason
WISDOM

Spirited
part
anger
COURAGE

JUSTICE is the wise regulation of anger/ ambition and appetite/lust.

Appetite
desire
MODERATION

Psyche can be seen to have three parts due to endo-psychic conflict.

Each part has its own function.

Parts may function well or poorly. Excellence in function is virtue.

Three parts correspond to three social classes, which each have their own work.

The head function should lead, letting wisdom regulate desires and passion.

The unjust soul is led by ignorance, which is manifest as cowardice, foolhardiness, gluttony, or lust

BEND YOUR MIND

Mind as Consciousness (er… Language)

I am. My mind exists. This first metaphysical theorem of Descartes withstood all his efforts to doubt it, since by doubting he was thinking, and if he was thinking, he existed.

But what is this mind? Having shown that the mind exists, Descartes next had to show what it was. What is the essential nature of the mind? What is its defining attribute, the capacity that makes it what it is? (By relying at this crucial juncture on a notion of essence, Descartes shows his continuing debt to the ancient Greek idea of substantial forms. In the beginning of the modern, there is an ancient inheritance.)

Because he knows he exists, but he is not yet sure of the external world, Descartes concludes that mind must exist independently of body. And since thought as such is all that is inseparable from himself, the essence of mind must be *consciousness* itself (inclusive of thought, doubt, sensations, awareness, dreams, imagination, etc.). The mind is a *thinking* thing (*res cogitans*), an entity with private awareness as its inner nature.

"But what then am I? A thing that thinks. What is that? A thing that doubts, understands, affirms, denies, wills, refuses, and that also imagines and senses."

—Descartes, Meditation II

For Descartes, thought is also what makes us distinct from animals. Animals are non-conscious automata. He wrote (carefully), "All the actions of beasts are similar only to those which we perform without the help of our minds" (*Fourth Replies*). Indeed, many of our actions are automatic, mechanical, habitual, or reflexive, requiring no consciousness. It is our use of words to express thoughts that makes us unique. Animals can't comment.

So Descartes' use of "thought" is ambiguous: sometimes it means any old conscious awareness; sometimes, it is bound up with language.

Mind-Bending Psychophysics

In a quiet movie hall, it is easy to hear people whispering several seats away from you. In a loud bar room, it is hard to be heard even while shouting. Here the background noise drowns out even a loud shout. Yet in silence, a slight whisper is impossible to ignore.

We can notice smaller differences at lower volumes, while at high volumes larger differences are required before they can be noticed over the din. The *just noticeable difference* is small in quiet environments, large in loud ones.

Imagine you are in a dark room, looking at a small lamp attached to a finely graduated dimmer switch. Someone turns the switch slightly, and records whether you notice any change in the brightness of the bulb. This dimmer switch shows the exact amount of electrical energy being consumed in producing light of a given intensity. When the bulb is dim, small changes in the input energy will be

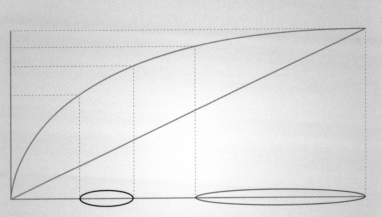

The horizontal axis indicates a physical quantity (amount of energy consumed at a given setting of the dimmer switch), while the vertical axis records a mental or subjective factor (through observer reports). Each higher stage on the vertical axis marks a smaller noticeable increment in brightness.

readily noticeable to you. But when the bulb is bright, the switch will have to be rotated much more before a difference in brightness is observable. Small input changes will be imperceptible. Once again, the size of the *just noticeable difference* depends on the intensity of the standard or comparison stimulus.

Gustav Fechner (1801–87) was a German mystic and physicist who sought to unite mind and body in one mathematical law. Mathematics was no longer only for the study of the external world. He found a mathematical formula to express the above observations about subjectively noticeable differences. Mapped out, his formula gives a graph that looks like the one shown above.

To notice that a low light has become brighter than it appeared at first, the dimmer switch must go up by a small amount (the blue circle). This is like the whisper across a quiet room. To notice an increase in brightness relative to the midpoint, the dimmer must be turned up by a large amount (red circle). Since energy costs money, this is also an argument for low-energy light bulbs.

If our senses were perfect, we would notice the slightest change in input energy, and our response curve would be a straight line (see diagonal on chart). The bend in the actual response curve shows the active power of the mind, Fechner concluded.

Fechner rejected Descartes' substance dualism in favor of *psycho-physical parallelism*, the view that mind and matter were dual aspects of the same underlying substance or reality. In fact, as a *panpsychist*, Fechner believed that psyche existed in everything.

MIND YOUR HEAD

Hume: Mine, not Me

David Hume famously doubted Descartes' indubitable first principle, *I think, therefore I am*. For Descartes, this was a sure-fire proof of the existence of the mind or soul (the *I*). But Hume observed that all he could find within were so many ideas, immediate impressions, or reflections based on these. Which idea (which object of your thought or feeling) is your self? The self is only a theater of appearing ideas:

"For my part, when I enter most intimately into what I call myself, I always stumble upon some particular perception or other, of heat or cold, light or shade, love or hatred, pain or pleasure. I can never catch myself at any time without a perception, and never can observe anything but the perception."
–Hume's *Treatise*, Bk I, Pt IV, Sc. VI

In short, there are thoughts, but no thinker. We "are nothing but a bundle or collection of different perceptions, which succeed each other with an inconceivable rapidity, and are in a perpetual flux and movement." Later, the materialist physician, La Mettrie (1709–51), who published an infamous book, *Man, the Machine*, echoed this skepticism of self with another metaphor: "The soul is a candle whose flame is relit the moment it is put out." Both views are close in spirit, wording, and metaphor to the Buddhist doctrine of selflessness (*anatman*), though without a yoga or meditative discipline intended to root out the self habit.

Kant: I Am Beyond All That

The absence of the self as an immediate object of intuition is not the end of the story. What unites Hume's bundle of perceptions together, making them more than a heap or a scattering? And all my experiences are indeed united, in so far as they are all *mine*. My experiences all bear reference to the self they do not reveal.

You may casually say that you are a totally different person than you were when you were four years old. Still, it was you who had all those experiences back then, or they wouldn't be your memories now.

For Immanuel Kant, the unity of personal experience proved there was a

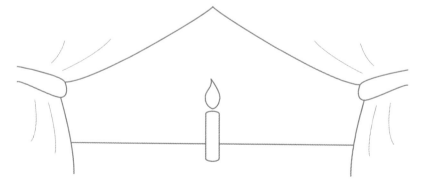

self, but a self that transcended its own experience while uniting it. We know ourselves as one only in reflective thought, not as an immediate intuition. Yet this *transcendental unity* is necessary, not random or accidental. The self *as it is in itself* is not revealed in the self *as it appears to itself.*

To test Kant's necessity claim, consider the following (admittedly unlikely) event. You are taking stock of all your mental contents, rummaging through your reminiscences, sorting your feelings and thoughts like wares in the storehouse of your mind. Quite unexpectedly, you come across one of *my* ideas. This is not simply your perfect grasp of what I meant, but literally my idea occurring in your mind. (Give it back!)

If you think this scenario is not just wildly implausible, but *a priori* impossible, you may have Kantian leanings.

Huxley: What Does Consciousness Do?

For Descartes, consciousness exists within a point, wholly without geometrical extension (yet capable of geometrical thought). Independent of all spatial extension, mind is literally *no place.* (John Locke replied to this by saying in effect that wherever he goes, his mind goes with him.)

T. H. Huxley (1825–95) championed the view that consciousness was merely an effect, never a cause. Consciousness—like a cast shadow—does nothing at all. Your subjective experiences come about due to physiological causes, but your consciousness of them is a mere witness, a "helpless spectator." It can suffer, but can affect nothing. Rather than denying the existence of consciousness outright, this

strategy grants its existence but denies its efficacy. In Huxley's famous phrase, "We are conscious automata."

James: "Breath Moving Outward"

Huxley's impotent ghost in a physiological machine was anathema to the pragmatism of William James (see pp. 118–119).

Why, James wondered, does consciousness appear during hesitation and indecision, and disappear under habit? It must have some function connected with decision and action. Apart from this function, it was no *thing*, not an entity at all. Yet, on further analysis, there was something more:

"... I am as confident as I am of anything that, in myself, the stream of thinking ... is only a careless name for what, when scrutinized, reveals itself to consist chiefly of the stream of my breathing. The 'I think' which Kant said must be able to accompany all my objects, is the 'I breathe' which actually does accompany them. ... breath, which was ever the original of 'spirit,' breath moving outwards, between the glottis and the nostrils, is, I am persuaded, the essence out of which philosophers have constructed the entity known to them as consciousness."
—James, 1904

THE PROBLEM:

Imagine a future neuroscientist called Mary who knows everything about color vision. She knows everything that physics can teach us about physical objects, including how they interact with light, and how light enters the human eye and is processed in the brain. However, she is color-blind and has never actually seen color. She has seen lemons and knows that they are yellow, but she has never seen yellow, nor seen lemons to be yellow.

One day Mary's color vision is repaired. When she opens up her eyes after the operation, how will she respond? Given her expertise, will she be able to identify and distinguish colors, one from another? If she is handed a blue lemon as a practical joke, will she be fooled?

THE METHOD:

It has been stated that how one answers this question about Mary can reveal one's underlying metaphysical assumptions. Let's see how.

Frank Jackson, who created the original ancestor of this problem, thought Mary would indeed be surprised, and he used this conclusion to argue against physicalism. Physicalism means many things to many philosophers, from "everything real is physical," to "every mental event is a physical event" to "every statement is equivalent in meaning with some physical statement." "Materialism" is its disputed synonym. Jackson's argument was that since Mary knew all the physical facts about color, her surprise shows there are non-physical facts to know about color. These include private facts like the raw feel of color, the way it looks to one who sees it, the subjective quality of color experience, or what philosophers call its quale (pronounced kwa-lay, plural qualia). What post-surgical Mary picks up, and which even the most comprehensive and accurate physical theories would have to miss, are color qualia—for instance, the blueness of blue, the redness of red, and so on.

It may be obvious to you that, if Mary has never seen colors, then her vaunted mastery of the sciences of color will be unable to fill the gap. Color cannot be explained to the color-blind, any more than sound can be shown to the deaf. Yet it is quite possible to agree that Mary would be surprised without believing color experience is non-physical, irreducibly subjective, or even radically private.

On the other hand, it is also possible to think that Mary's surprise is unlikely, even absurd. If Mary knew everything there was to know about color, she had to know what color looked like.

THE SOLUTION:

It is important not to get our imaginary facts wrong. No one said Mary knew everything there is to know about color, only everything physical sciences can determine regarding color. Thus the question becomes whether everything that can be known about color can be shown by physical sciences. Can qualia, for instance, in any sense be known through purely physicalistic neuroscience?

Here is one way to argue that Mary would have known what colors look like, even had she never seen them. By hypothesis, Mary has never seen color, and we are presumably to take this literally. But isn't it possible that Mary could have imagined colors without ever having actually seen any? Never having seen a color is not at all equivalent to never having imagined it.

Suppose Mary's defect filters all information for color as it exits the eyes, so that her color-processing areas are intact. Suppose she invents a machine that stimulates color-processing areas of her brain in patterns that match the brains of people seeing color. This stimulation creates varied color experiences in Mary, so that she, despite never having seen color, can soon imagine colors at will. But whenever she turned from her colorful imaginings to look out upon the external world, she could only see shades of gray.

One might object that this innovation violates the terms of the original problem, since we do say that those who hallucinate "see lights and colors and images that are not there," and Mary is supposed never to have seen colors. But this sense of the verb "to see" is obviously distinct from the literal interpretation we presumed to take. Let the distinction be granted as just, but then so what? How would Mary ever know which colors have the names we color-sighted people give them? Even if she had "seen" cobalt blue in her mind's eye, she would not know it was blue, let alone which blue it was, still less what to call it. So after the operation she would say: "So, that color is cobalt blue!"

This new objection forgets that Mary is omniscient about color science. A simple extension of her machine will allow her to know that the artificially-generated color experience she is currently having is not the one people have when they look at yellow lemons. She will know that her current brain state, and the color experience it produces, is the same as the brain state of an individual who is looking at cobalt blue. So Mary will easily recognize, based on neuroscience alone, that the subjective experience of color she is now having is likely to be cobalt blue, so that this lemon before her is a gag.

THE PHILOSOPHER'S GOD

The Ontological Argument No. 1

One classic argument for God's existence turns on an ingenious definition of God as that greater than which cannot be conceived. The definition is carefully worded so as to be neutral on the question of whether or not we can conceive God. That is only prudent when attempting to define or circumscribe the Absolute.

So defined—the argument goes—God must exist. We can certainly conceive of something existing, and we can grant that to exist is greater than not to exist. So if God were merely possible, and did not actually exist, we could conceive of something greater still, namely that possible God actually existing. So God is not merely possible, God exists.

The Ontological Argument No. 2

The ontological argument has also been put another way. God is a being possessing all the perfections. Existence is a perfection. So God exists.

The argument attracts philosophers because it proceeds *a priori*. It assumes nothing about the universe, only about conceivability. It also assumes that the definition is logically consistent, that is, that it is at least possible for there to be something greater than which cannot be conceived. The skeptic must be exceptionally uncharitable to claim that so great a thing is utterly impossible.

In the ontological argument, God's existence is derived from his definition. If the definition may be presumed to encapsulate the essence of God, we can say that God's essence includes his existence. God exists by his very nature.

QUESTION

If the existence of God is a necessary truth, what is the nature of that necessity? Is the necessity physical, logical, or ethical? Or is God his own modality?

THE HISTORICAL PERSPECTIVE

The ontological argument crops up many times in the history of philosophy after St. Anselm (1033–1109) introduced it into theology. Descartes, for instance (after he had doubted all he could and at last found his first indubitable principle, the existence of the self), struck out from that slender basis alone to reconstruct the entire world. The first big step in that direction is his proof of the existence of God. While he is yet certain only of the existence of his own mind and its various contents, Descartes happens upon a concept of God amid his ideas. From this concept alone, Descartes' subjective definition of God, he proves the existence of God. How does he do it? The definition is much the same as Anselm's. God's essence, so defined, implies his existence.

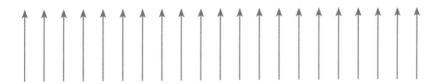

God or Gods?

If God is that greater than which we cannot conceive, it would follow that we cannot conceive of anything greater. But could not the great be ranked in their own right, beyond our conception? As in mathematics, it is one thing to prove existence, quite another to prove uniqueness. One might grant Anselm his self-existent deity, and then wonder what else is up that sleeve.

Gaunilo, a monk of Anselm's time, wondered whether the same reasoning did not imply the existence of an island greater than which cannot be conceived. This most perfect island would be less than can be conceived without existing. Gaunilo intended this repartee as a counter-argument. Perhaps it ought rather to be taken as an open invitation to polytheists: can the boundless be contained in one brow?

God as an Absolutely Infinite Substance

Spinoza also introduces God by definition. God is a "substance consisting of infinite attributes, each of which expresses eternal and infinite essence." In other words, God has infinitely many essential attributes, each infinite in its own right. Each essence must be conceived through itself and is ultimately self-caused. So God is self-caused, his essence involves his existence.

Two of these attributes are thinking and extension. So Spinoza's God is infinitely extended. Indeed, our thoughts and even our bodies are but finite modes expressing these divine essences, expressing "God or Nature." In the words of the Grateful Dead tune, "wake up to discover that you are the eyes of the world."

EXISTENCE IS NO PREDICATE

To conceive of something is already to conceive of it existing. To imagine Santa Claus is to imagine Santa Claus existing. To believe in the tooth fairy is to believe the tooth fairy exists. The conception may be empty, the imagination pure, and the belief false. But to exist is not part of being conceived or imagined or believed in. Put differently, existence is not a predicate. To treat existence as predicate is to imagine it can enhance a concept by being added to it (as you enhance your concept of my bike when you learn that it is red). In the context of Anselm's argument, it is only an illicit way to sneak the conclusion in amongst the premises. The resulting circularity—according to Kant's critique of Anselm—is the logical sin of the ontological argument.

DID GOD SING THE UNIVERSE?

OM resonates in space, and the world is all vibration. Its fundamental frequency is the vibe you want to be on, but to find this key—it turns out—spelling is everything. You'd think it would be easy to spell OM—not at all! That belly-resonant chant is said to be the origin of all sounds—of all syllables, the universal sound, the first word of the world. Remarkable powers are attributed to this divine utterance, beginning with its remarkable spelling.

How to Spell OM

OM is spelled with four letters (or *sounds*): AUM_, where the _ stands for the necessary silence that ends the word. The A is the whisper of aspiration before the U (the well-rounded sound that can be breathlessly prolonged), followed by a slow closing of the lips in M as breath runs out. OM is chanted for as long as possible, so no doubt it became necessary to add the silence afterwards so that the yogis could finally inhale again, and prepare for the next round.

The four letters also serve as a mnemonic device, applied as a fourfold schema to represent all manner of things. A is the past, U the present, M the future, and the silence the timeless beyond. Or: A is the origin, U the preservation, M is the destruction of the world, the fourth being eternal silence into which all is resolved, only to be born again (for the Indian universe is an endless series of worlds, one after another). All three sounds are but references to aspects of an impersonal primordial absolute being (*brahman*). Time is a word, all nature a divine chant.

Consciousness Has Four Conditions

The initial A also represents your waking consciousness, everyday consciousness, with the senses turned outwards. This is the common condition of all. Engaged or distracted, the ego is present, immersed in sensoriphysical reality and yet apart from it.

The second letter U stands for the consciousness of dreams, those inner interruptions of sleep in which the senses turn on—only *inwardly*—enacting past deeds, present desires, or wishful futures. You are present in your dream as you confront the dream-world, but you are also the dreamer, the dream-maker, the world-maker of your dream. Only, in your dream, you may not know that. You are both. This becomes clear when you wake up.

M is deep sleep, without dream and without desire—without mind, without separateness, without sense of self. Here the flittering ego is not present. Here abides an undisturbed stillness, a limitless depth, an infinite peace. M is that all-powerful world-maker, that all-knowing ruler that presides in the hearts of all, the artificer of dreams. In this darkness sleeps the source and end of all.

Now Quietly…

The silence at the end of OM is the silent recognition in meditation that you are that source. Who you really are is the fourth world-dreaming silence, the universal consciousness of *brahman*. It is a knowing without parts, beyond both the senses and the intellect, beyond birth, even, and death. To know it is to know joy. The fourth is *atman*, your true self. But *atman* is *brahman*. Thou art that. *Atman* is within; *brahman* is beyond. The beyond is within. Transcend inwardly.

Lucid Living

The self can be realized through a meditative process of slowing down and even ceasing everyday consciousness, sinking awareness ever deeper into an inward calm, preserving consciousness through an inner stillness equal to that of sleep. The passionate disturbances as in dreams also afflict the meditator, but these too are quieted by perseverance. The realization of the world-maker is an ancient but frank call for that inner mastery known today as lucid dreaming. (Lucid dreaming is a dream in which you know you are dreaming.) To make the world is really just to project everyday consciousness. To realize you make your world is really just to do so lucidly.

GOOD GOD!

Getting to Know God

People's conception of God, including God's purposes and essential nature, vary widely. Even atheists must deny existence to a God of a particular description. Perhaps it is vain to define God, to try to reduce God to a name. But it seems hard to believe or to disbelieve without doing so.

Those who come to know God are regularly impressed by his majesty and power. Arguably, the idea of power is essential to the idea of an absolute being, He Who Holds all the Cards. The omnipotence of God is dear to the hearts of many believers. It also has a totalitarian connotation to some of God's critics. Without denying divine omnipotence, many believers will offset this one-sided epithet with more cautious, even opposing attributes, such as the suffering of God, his proximity to the downtrodden and the powerless, the possibility of hope. Thus it is sometimes said that God is not to be understood in positive and human terms, but only through opposites, through negatives and dialectic.

Another divine attribute routinely stressed by those who believe in their hearts is beneficence, omnibenevolence, the absolute and pure Goodness of God. This is Good on God's own terms, which we can but glimpse in human terms. God's Good is not easy to understand. None can scrutinize the Inscrutable Plan. We may rack our heads to understand; we may find some comfort in related sacred verses; we may seek the counsel of those we consider closer to God than ourselves. Rarely will we be advised in this case to understand God in negative or opposing terms

(although once again the compassionate suffering of God is a telling dialectical theological rejoinder).

QUESTION

Could God create something so heavy that even he could not move it?

The Definition of Evil

One might define evil curtly as suffering (as, indeed, utilitarians do). In this sense, God might even be said by some believers to visit evil upon his enemies, whose suffering would then count as divine justice, rather than a wrong. Divine or not, retribution is not love. Alternatively, one can define evil as unnecessary suffering.

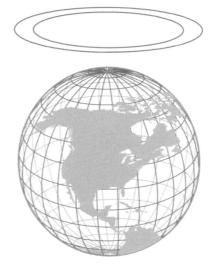

The drawback of this definition is that it presumes one is in a position to distinguish necessity from vanity. In fact, much unnecessary suffering is due to human-on-human violence.

Today even natural-looking disasters like hurricanes, floods, and lightning-ignited forest fires may have human causes (like climate change) as part of their complex etiologies. Still, all of these, like earthquakes and tsunamis (even when emergency preparation and response is excellent) cause widespread suffering of innocent people. It is hard to see how suffering so senseless can be necessary.

In any case, the widespread prevalence of senseless suffering makes the actual world appear to be fundamentally unjust or at least, as French writer and philosopher Albert Camus put it, "benignly indifferent." Bliss in the next world is hardly compensation, any more than Job's second family is a compensation for the loss of his first.

THE PROBLEM OF EVIL

The existence of evil is notorious. Why does unnecessary suffering exist? If God were all-powerful, he could prevent it. If God were all-good, he would. Since it exists, he either can't or won't prevent it. Power and purity seem to part company at their upper limit. The dilemma posed by evil is this: God is either limited and all good, or all-powerful but not wholly good.

Question: If there were no malevolent free spirit in the universe, credit for unnecessary suffering (not caused by humans) would have to fall to an almighty God. Does God need his Adversary *in order* to be good?

QUESTION

Could God create spirits so evil that even he could not love them?

The first truth of Buddhism is that all is suffering (*dukkha*, from a Pali word with the literal meaning "out of joint" (like a shoulder) or "broken" (like an axle). The world is a rough ride. The world is fundamentally unsatisfactory. It is easy to read this as a plain statement of the existence of unnecessary and unjustified suffering, in short, as the problem of the existence of evil. Although thirst, craving, and hence karma are involved in suffering arising, the Buddha does not pin individual suffering on private past-life deeds. He does not, in other words, blame the victims. As the saying goes: good karma, spread it around; bad karma, spread it around. The world is not fair.

ULTIMATE CHOICES

Let us suppose that I offer you two options, A and B, and you have to choose one. I tell you that if you choose A you could win eternal bliss or you may be wasting a little time and effort. If you choose B you will have some fun in the short term, but you could spend perpetuity suffering the torture of the damned. I can't tell you the odds, but these are the possible outcomes of your decision. Which of these do you choose? Give this a moment's thought before you read on.

Pascal's Wager

With the case stated in this way, you would have to be insane to take the risk of choosing an option that could bring you infinite harm but offers finite benefits over one that might have a small cost but could bring infinite benefits. This being so, reasoned the 17th-century French philosopher Blaise Pascal, why would anyone choose not to believe in God? Even if you have no faith, even if you can find no rational proof of his existence, Christianity—said Pascal—has got to be the best bet, given what you stand to gain by belief and what you stand to lose by non-belief.

So what are you waiting for? Start believing, if you don't already. Which brings us to the first of many criticisms of Pascal's position. Can one choose to believe? Surely belief in something must be founded upon an inkling of its truth. Can belief spring from a fear-based calculation? Can faith be a bet?

The American philosopher William James, in his important paper entitled *Will to Believe* (1896), thought otherwise, saying "We feel that a faith in masses and holy water adopted willfully after such a mechanical calculation lacks the inner soul of faith's reality; and if we were of the Deity, we should probably take pleasure in cutting off believers from their infinite reward." So you might try to adopt the belief, but you won't fool God.

The Will to Believe

James went on in his paper to argue that—at least under some conditions—it is *perfectly rational* to let emotion and desire influence our choice of beliefs. The conditions are limited, but many moral, interpersonal, religious questions qualify.

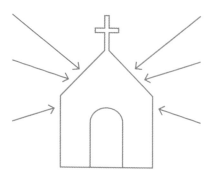

To see this, consider that options may be of several kinds. *Classified relative to the person who is to make the choice*, options may be:

1. living or dead
2. forced or avoidable
3. momentous or trivial.

For options that are *living, forced, and momentous*, James deemed it logically permissible to allow one's "passional nature" to influence one's choices.

Living means relevant, in the realm of the possible, *relative to the one choosing*. *Forced* means unavoidable. *Momentous* implies a significant, irreversible choice involving unique opportunities.

"Does God exist or not?"—this formulation is easily avoidable, since one can be an agnostic. "Should I believe in God or not?"—this question is quite unavoidable (provided one is live to the God issue at all). With regard to forced options, James pointed out that "When you have to make a choice and don't make it, that is in itself a choice."

Here's another question that meets James' three conditions: *Is life worth living?* This issue cannot be settled by scientific investigation. On the contrary, your belief, one way or another, can have an impact on the answer. Said James, "Believe that life is worth living and your belief will help create the fact." Believe otherwise, and you just may make it so.

HOW HIGH THE MOON?

"Can I be successful?" This question disturbs many a self-doubter. Of course, you don't know if you don't try. But the answer you take with you into the trial may affect the outcome. Under these conditions, "Belief creates the actual fact." James's conclusion? "There are, then, cases where a fact cannot come at all unless a preliminary faith exists in its coming."

Some things we must believe if they will be true.

Social trust, friendship, goodwill, and other acts of humanity also have the potential (sorry, no guarantee) to be self-fulfilling prophecies. But James also throws some basic metaphysical issues up for emotional grabs when he writes:

"We can act as if there were a God; feel as if we were free; consider Nature as if she were full of special designs; lay plans as if we were to be immortal; and we find then that these words do make a genuine difference in our moral life."

GAUTAMA THE BUDDHA

Born the son of a king, Siddhartha Gautama led a privileged life without ugliness or suffering. But he emerged from this protected innocence after encountering sickness, age, and death, which he could see were miseries. After the custom in ancient India, he forsook his home life and retired to the forests to find out the truth of things and overcome thereby death and infirmity. Hermit yogis taught him expanded and transcendent mental states. Later still, ascetics taught him fasting and other body-conquering techniques. He mastered them all, but found himself no closer to the ultimate truth and final liberation he was seeking.

The Path to Enlightenment

So he set out on a middle path between the seductions of comfort and those of self-sacrifice. He sat comfortably under a tree and brought awareness to the present moment, notably the subtle sensations throughout the body, which constantly accompany daily existence, so regularly in fact that we can almost forget they are there.

These sensations change with our emotions and react in response to circumstances and to our own internal chatter. Sometimes they are intensely painful, other times highly pleasant. Unless we fix our attention on them, our habitual patterns of reaction will predominate, which means we will be driven by passions, battered by disappointments, seething with regrets or frustrated hopes; in other words, we will be our usual selves.

Through a practice of mindful awareness of bodily sensations, whether pleasant or unpleasant, together with an imperturbable equanimity or mental poise of *mere observation*, one destroys old reaction patterns (past karma), and regains one's natural liberation. Standing midway between pain or pleasure, this mental balance counteracts the craving and aversion that overcome us from moment to moment. That night, Siddhartha followed this middle path to the final goal, *nirvana*, which is liberation from suffering. By daybreak he was a Buddha, One who is Awake.

Self as Illusion

The premise of the Buddha is that the world is out of kilter. Suffering is endemic, part of every life story. He was not blaming the victim when he said that the cause of suffering is craving, an ignorant clinging and thirst for life. We want what we do not have. We have what we do not want. The clamoring self is at the root of these frustrations, but the self is only a fiction of our life narratives. It is a rhetorical device we use to bind ourselves up with the world and to our relations. Our mental dramas intensify the suffering; stepping back from them relieves it. This does not require leaving home, or even withdrawing from experience. On the contrary, the posture of *just observing* is stepping back enough, and development of this mental discipline (or *yoga*) brings one closer to experience, ultimately liberating one by weakening reflexive habit patterns based on the illusion of self.

From Selflessness to Compassion

The Buddha's doctrine of no-self is a shocking reversal of the prevailing Indian wisdom, that *atman* is *brahman*, or Thou art That. This doctrine taught that our ultimate identity (*atman* = self) was one with God (*brahman* is the impersonal absolute). But the Buddha steered clear of these disputes. His argument was an invitation to look for yourself. What you will find where you expected your self is intricate interdependencies linking all forms and walks of life. There is no independent self, but a web of mutual arising, a network of reciprocal need. Like equanimity, the practices of compassion are corrosive to all selfish tendencies. In practice, the proof of realization of no-self lies in selfless altruism, in service to others. Enlightenment is not an epistemic enterprise only; ethics is inseparable from wisdom.

QUOTH THE BUDDHA

"What we are today comes from our thoughts of yesterday, and our present thoughts build our life of tomorrow: our life is the creation of the mind."
—*Dhammapada*, I, I

"It is within this fathom-long carcass, with its mind and its notions, that I declare there is the world, the origin of the world, the cessation of the world, and the path leading to the cessation of the world."
—*Samyutta Nikya*, I, 62

"I have gone round in vain the cycles of many lives, ever striving to find the builder of the house of life and death. How great is the sorrow of life that must die.

But now I have seen thee, house-builder: never more shalt thou build this house. The rafters of sin are broken, the ridge-pole of ignorance is destroyed. The fever of craving is past: for my mortal mind is gone to the joy of the immortal nirvana."
—*Dhammapada*, XI, 153–4

Logic and Infinity

Logic is the study and norms of good reasoning.
We look at the technical basics of logic, and at the
logic of words like "if," "and," "not," "all," "some,"
and "or." We can use such little words as these to
define some very big ideas, such as infinity, which
poses questions too big even for the previous
chapter. Here we tell many a tall tale in the service
of making the mathematics of infinity accessible
to finite minds, such as our own. We also survey
a range of *impossibilia*, paradoxes, and apparent
contradictions.

WHAT IS LOGIC?

We use the word "logical" to describe many things: a thought, a mind, even a seating arrangement. In philosophy, however, the adjective "logical" is applied in two specific contexts: a logical truth and a logical inference.

Logical truths are statements such as the following: *all bachelors are unmarried*; *triangles possess three sides*; *mammals are animals*; *seven is a number*. They are all not only true, but necessarily true. The price is that they say nothing new, and tend to ring a little hollow. The hope that logical truths are not all empty, but rather contain valuable surprise insights, has long powered philosophy.

An *inference* is a movement of thought from premises—the propositions put forward as the basis of an argument—to conclusion. Inferences have an if–then structure: *if this and that are true, then so is this other*. An inference always makes some assumptions, and always draws out some consequence.

An inference is an argument—not the shouting kind, but simply reasoning. Logic is the study of arguments. If you want a fancier name, call it the Science of Inference. It lays down principles as to what constitutes a good argument, a valid inference, a logical conclusion.

To call a conclusion logical is not to pay it a compliment, as if to say one had made a sensible arrangement of assumptions, like guests around a dinner table. In everyday speech, we may say of a plausible guess that it "sounds logical." But in philosophy, to call a conclusion logical is to say much more than that it may be a good guess.

First, in philosophy, a conclusion is logical *only relative* to a set of premises. Technically, it is not the conclusion itself that is logical, but its relation to the premises: it either *logically follows* from the premises, or it does not. It is the inference that is logical, not usually the conclusion on its own. Only a logical truth follows validly from any arbitrary set of premises! A necessary truth is true no matter what, so any inference to a logical truth will be valid. This is another way to say that it is very easy to prove the obvious.

To follow logically from one set of premises does not confer a permanent status on a conclusion. The same statement may follow from one set of assumptions, but not from another.

In an inference, you are permitted to make your assumptions. But thereafter you have to keep them, or else abandon both the inference and the conclusion at once.

This relativity has an upside: A bad argument is never the end of an argument. If suddenly you realize that your argument holds no water, and cannot stand, don't give up! There may be better arguments that do support your position. A conclusion illogical by one route may be logical by another.

When you have examined all the arguments in favor of your position, and you find it still holds no water, welcome to philosophy! It's time to change your mind.

EXERCISES

Philosophers who study logic have introduced a raft of technical meanings for terms that are ordinarily used in quite different senses. Some of the differences between philosophical and ordinary language are shown below.

In this table, you find on the left various expressions occurring commonly in dialogue and debate. Below are alternatives that respect philosophical conventions. Arguably, no expression has any meaning torn from its context, as the common expressions in this table have been. So translation is out of the question. No attempt is made here to give the meaning of the common expression as it occurs (say) in your next philosophical discussion. But the common expressions on the left are often used in ways that violate the conventions of philosophy-speak. In some contexts only, what is meant by them will match the expressions on the right. These are less likely to earn you the censure of the over-educated.

A logical conclusion!	A valid inference!
What is your point?	What is your conclusion? (Which proposition are you trying to support?)
His argument is that the poor should benefit most.	His major premise (or perhaps top priority) is that the poor should benefit most.
He made some good arguments, but his logic was faulty.	He mentioned some relevant considerations (premises), but his argument was invalid. The conclusion does not follow from his assumptions.
Her conclusion was wrong.	The evidence (premises) she cited supported a different conclusion.
His reasoning was sound but his conclusion was wrong.	His argument was valid, but his premises were false. (Explanation: if the argument is valid, and the conclusion is false, then at least one of the premises must be false.)
I can't accept your conclusion.	Either your premises are false or your argument is invalid.
He just kept saying the same thing.	His reasoning was circular. He failed to consider the relevance of other evidence.
His perspective was valid.	His perspective was welcome (socially rather than logically.)

WHAT MAKES A GOOD ARGUMENT?

Logic is the analysis and appraisal of arguments. An argument is an attempt to advance a position by providing reasons as support. The reasons are premises; the position to be supported is the conclusion. An argument is the basis of an inference from premises to a conclusion.

Arguments can be more or less successful. That is, they can offer strong or weak support for their conclusion. The same conclusion can be supported by many arguments, some better than others. The same set of premises constitutes strong support for one conclusion, but weak support for another. It is the business of logic to discern the difference between strong and weak support, to clarify what makes arguments good, bad, or abysmal.

The first step in logical analysis is identifying the premises and the conclusion. This is not always easy. Premises are often presumed without a word and taken for granted. They literally go without saying, often because they seem so obvious to the person making the argument. They may appear less obvious, even false, to the person at whom the argument is directed.

Skill in logic enables one to recognize that a premise is being tacitly assumed. One recognizes holes in arguments where the premises ought to be.

Identifying the conclusion is usually more straightforward, but not always. For one thing, the conclusion of one argument may be a premise in the next argument, forming a chain of reasoning. There is nothing inherent in any proposition that makes it a premise or a conclusion; these are roles that propositions play in context. Sometimes, the conclusion itself is left unstated, although usually that only happens when it is unpalatable or somehow impolite to say. One is presented with premises selected and arranged so as to point in the same direction. Like the movie that ends with a kiss, you know what is to come, but it is never shown or said.

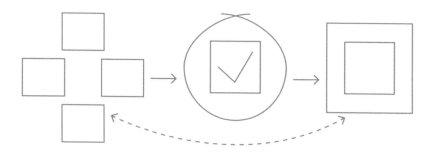

Validating an Argument

The second step in logical analysis is evaluation of the argument, determining its overall strength. This is where questions of validity and soundness arise. There are three primary criteria to consider: the relevance, the acceptability, and the sufficiency of the premises, always relative to a specified conclusion.

Criterion 1

The requirement of *relevance* may be simply stated: the premises must be, directly or indirectly, *about the conclusion*. From premises about cats, nothing follows about dogs. Often premises offered as reasons are not directly about the concepts in the conclusion, but usually they can be *made relevant indirectly* by articulating linking premises. From premises about yesterday, nothing follows about today, but if we add a premise that links past and present, relevance may be achieved, and reasoning strengthened.

Failures of relevance sometimes arise because people are confused. More often, the reasons given are relevant indirectly in virtue of unstated assumptions. To be logical thinkers, we must be sensitive to unstated assumptions, or we may miss the relevance of the reasons being advanced. Logic requires listening.

Criterion 2

Premises must also be *acceptable*. Put simply, they must be true or probable. A set of premises may be sufficient for a conclusion, but if one or more of them is a known falsehood, the argument will persuade no one. *The basic idea of an argument is to lead thinking from truth to truth.* If there is no warrant for the premises, their relevance and sufficiency will transfer zero warrant to the conclusion. You can't prove anything from false premises.

However, it is common in philosophy to contemplate hypothetically, to think as *if* certain premises were true.

The very mark of an educated mind, according to Aristotle, is the ability to entertain an idea without accepting it. What ultimately makes premises acceptable is a profound imponderable, which we consider elsewhere under the headings of Truth, Value, and Necessity.

Criterion 3

Reasons may be acceptable and relevant but still not enough. They must also be *sufficient* for the conclusion. What counts as sufficient depends on circumstances and needs. The highest grade of sufficiency is called *(deductive) validity*. Here the truth of the premises ensures the truth of the conclusion. Sufficiency is 100%. In a valid argument, it is literally impossible for the premises to be true and the conclusion false. The Paradigms of Reason presented in the next section are all examples of this gold standard of sufficiency. Mathematics requires deductive validity in all its proofs. In philosophy, validity is a veritable fetish.

PARADIGMS OF REASON

There are many ways to argue well, and many valid argument forms. This section offers three classics. All three examples are valid arguments, despite having false premises. To be valid, the conclusion must follow from the assumption of the premises. Supposing the premises to be true, the conclusion is as well.

A sound argument, by contrast, is a valid argument that has true premises. In examples 2 and 3, the first premise is not only false, but a manipulative ploy, one romantic, the other political. Valid reasoning is not enough. Truth flows from truth, not from assumption.

Example 1: Modus Ponens

If an animal has hair, then it is a mammal. This animal has hair, therefore it is a mammal.

$$\frac{\text{If P, then Q} \quad \text{P}}{\text{Therefore, Q}}$$

Example 2: Denying the Consequent

If you loved me, then you'd take me to the movies. You are not taking me to the movies, so you must not love me.

$$\frac{\text{If P, then Q} \quad \text{Not-Q}}{\text{Therefore, Not-P}}$$

Example 3: Disjunctive Syllogism

You're either with us, or you're against us! You're not with us, so you must be against us.

$$\frac{\text{Either P or Q} \quad \text{Not P}}{\text{Therefore, Q}}$$

ANSWERS

Explanation 1

The if–then premise is called a *conditional*. Example 1 says that P is a *sufficient condition* for Q to be true. The second premise then says that this sufficient condition is met. You can also read the first premise as saying that Q is a *necessary condition* of P. That's why Q *necessarily* follows from these two premises, making this a valid argument.

This argument is also called *Affirming the Antecedent* (the antecedent is the if-clause).

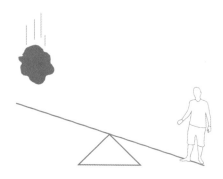

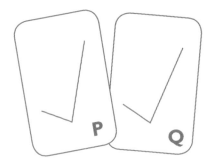

Explanation 2

In Denying the Consequent, the first premise is the same as before. Again, it says P is sufficient for Q. Q would be true if only P were. But Q isn't true, according to the second premise. So P can't be true either. Indeed, no condition sufficient for Q can be true, if Q isn't.

The first premise of this second example might be equally expressed as a disjunction: "Either you take me to the movies or you don't love me." This form brings out the similarity to the next example (see also pp. 138–139).

Explanation 3

The first premise says that there are at most two alternatives. The second premise denies one of those. So only the other one remains.

The ancient Greek skeptic, Sextus Empiricus, reports a story of a dog achieving reason, by using a disjunctive syllogism with three possible alternatives.

A dog is "tracking an animal and comes to a meeting of three roads. After he has tried two of the roads and found that the animal has not passed that way, he rushes off immediately on the third without even stopping to pick up the scent." The dog reasons thus: "The animal passed either this way, or this way, or this way; but it did not take this road, nor that, therefore it must have gone by the third road."

If dogs can use a complex disjunctive syllogism, they can use logic. If they can use logic, they are capable of rational thought. If they are capable of rational thought, human beings are not the only rational animals.

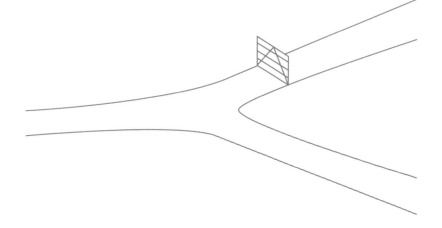

REDUCTION AND INDUCTION
(*reductio ad absurdum*)

If P, then the absurd is true

Therefore, P is not true

This is just like denying the consequent, but here the consequent denies itself, in being absurd. An absurdity is any statement that cannot possibly be true. The negation of a logical truth is absurd: *some bachelors are married*; *triangles are not shapes*.

Typically, this form of argument is used to refute an opponent's position. You assume what they assume, take their premises as your premises, and deduce a contradiction or other absurdity. (A contradiction is a statement that both affirms and denies the same position, and therefore cannot possibly be true.) *Reductio ad absurdum* is a way of arguing

that a position is logically incoherent, and so must be revised or dropped.

Most arguments require more than one premise. So, realistically, one assumes a whole set of premises (not just P, but P and Q and R, etc). But then, when you derive the contradiction, all you can conclude is that *at least one* of the premises is false. Ideally, all the premises but one are acceptable; in general, the chain of reasoning breaks at the weakest link (the shakiest premise).

A famous mathematical example of this style of argument shows that $\sqrt{2}$ is not a fraction. $\sqrt{2}$ is the square root of two—a number that, multiplied by itself, equals 2. A fraction is a ratio of counting numbers. You begin the proof by assuming that there

EXERCISES

Recognizing Logical Form

We've now looked at different kinds of premises and several different forms of arguments. Identify whether the following examples are arguments or mere assertions and express their logical form using Ps and Qs or other letters to symbolize the constituent propositions. Exercise 1 is completed as an example.

1. Unless you're going to the party, I'll see you at the swimming pool.

2. Anyone with any sense would buy the economy size. You bought the small one, so I guess you don't have any sense.

3. If it rains, the parade will be canceled. It is raining, so the parade will be canceled.

4. I know that all the fish in this river are salmon, because I've never caught anything else here.

5. An animal has hair if and only if it is a mammal.

Translate the arguments above into Ps and Qs. For example, 1 translates as "Either P or Q; if not P, then Q."

are indeed two whole numbers a and b, such that √2 =a/b. This assumption turns out to be absurd, in that you can derive a contradiction from it (namely, that a is both odd and even). The key point is that √2 is not a fraction, not a ratio of whole numbers. Put differently, √2 is an *irrational number*. That means that it can only be represented as an infinite, non-repeating decimal.

The philosophical significance of this mathematical *reductio* is discussed elsewhere (see Pythagoras, pp. 88–89).

Inductive Reasoning

I have a large can full of beads of various colors. I plunge my hand in and grab a fistful, and I find that half the beads in this sample are red. From this I conclude that half the beads in the can are red. Is my conclusion justified?

The inference of a generalization from a series of instances is something we do all the time. The process involves taking an instance (the minor premise) and, on the basis of the results of observations about that instance (the major premise), deriving a rule (the conclusion). "Snuggles is a cat. Snuggles likes eating fish. Therefore all cats like eating fish." Induction allows us to reach conclusions that go beyond what follows logically from the premises, but the price we pay is a level of uncertainty that

varies from that of opinion polls to that of scientific "facts." The truth of an inductive argument is not certain. It only has a probability of being true, and that probability depends on the degree to which—for example—Snuggles' behavior is typical of the class of cats.

Mathematical Induction

Imagine an infinitely long line of dominoes, each standing on its end. There is a first domino, and a next domino, and for every domino after that there is also a next domino. Assume they are all lined up in such a way that, if any one of them falls over, the next one will also fall over. Now knock the first one over. What can you conclude?

The answer is: they will all fall over. This conclusion follows logically. Despite its name, mathematical induction is a deductively valid argument. It is special because it gives us an orderly way to draw conclusions about infinitely many objects (usually numbers, but here dominoes).

ANSWERS

1. (Not an argument) If not the party, then the pool. If not P, then Q. Alternatively, P or Q. You party or we meet at the pool (but not both).

2. Denying the Consequent. If P then Q. But not Q (you bought small, not economy). Conclusion: Not P (you have no sense).

3. Affirming the Antecedent (*modus ponens*). If R, then no P. But R. Therefore, no parade.

4. A weak inductive argument, which might be made even weaker with better bait.

5. (Not an argument) If H, then M. If M, then H. Alternatively, either H and M, or neither H nor M.

Logic and Infinity   131

FALLACY SPOTTING

A fallacy is an argument that looks plausible, but relies on faulty reasoning. The word is derived from the Latin verb *fallere*, to deceive; deliberately using a fallacious argument is a bit like telling a lie. But we ourselves are the first victim of our unintentional fallacies.

A Question of Relevance

If a conclusion is to be drawn from premises, then those premises must be relevant—a premise must provide us with information that helps justify the conclusion. "Begging the question" is one way an argument can fail to do this. The heart of this fallacy lies in embedding the conclusion of an argument among the premises, *which ought to be supporting it.*

Circularity

In a circular argument, the same information is put forward both as a premise and as the conclusion, and this can be difficult to spot for the simple reason that the argument is a valid one. It is certainly true that if A then A, but no *reason is thereby given to believe A in the first place.*

Irrelevant Appeals

A premise might appeal to our sympathy, or to an authority that has no bearing on the subject matter, or might suggest that if we fail to agree then we are in some way at fault. None of these appeals is relevant to the substance of an argument. Children often use an argument known to philosophers as "Tu Quoque" (literally "You too"). While you might be accused of hypocrisy if you, a nail-biter, explain to your daughter why she should stop biting

hers, her response of "Well, you do it!" has no bearing on the validity of your case.

An *ad hominem* ("against the person") argument attacks the opponent or the character of the opponent rather than his or her argument. An extreme case of this is called "poisoning the well"—discrediting an opponent as a source so that others will reject any argument or information that he or she puts forward.

Premise Acceptability

"I know for a fact that different species can interbreed, because in my grandmother's home village there was a boy called Hootie whose father was an owl." Well, the information is relevant, and if true the evidence is overwhelming, but can we accept the premise? Arguments that are put forward with conviction can often blind us to the fact that the premises are—to say the least—shaky. It can be difficult to attack what may be a firmly held belief, but premises do need to be examined carefully, and even if we can't guarantee certainty we should demand probability.

Premise Set Insufficiency

"If an animal has hair, then it is a mammal. This animal has hair, therefore it is a mammal." As we have already seen, this form of argument—or syllogism—is valid. If you accept the premises, then you must accept the conclusion. To refute the conclusion, you would have to show either that not all animals with hair are mammals, or that the animal in question is hairless.

It is equally valid to argue "All mammals have hair. This animal doesn't have hair. Therefore it isn't a mammal." However, there are forms of syllogism that may sound reasonable enough but are in fact fallacious. For example, what can be inferred from the following premises?

QUESTION

No one is granted bail if he is held for murder. John isn't held for murder, therefore . . .
1. **He will be granted bail.**
2. **He won't be granted bail.**
3. **He is innocent.**
4. **None of these is a valid conclusion.**

It is tempting to conclude that John will be granted bail, but this argument is fallacious. Known as *denying the antecedent*, it takes the form "If A then B; not A, so not B." (If murder, then no bail; not murder, therefore bail.) We can't tell

from the premises whether or not he will be granted bail. He may be held for another crime for which bail is denied. For that matter, the premises do not even imply that John is being held! The answer is 4.

QUESTION

All mammals have hair. This animal has hair, therefore . . .
1. **It is a mammal.**
2. **It is not a mammal.**
3. **Not all mammals have hair.**
4. **None of these is a valid conclusion.**

Again, the first option yields an invalid argument. It takes the form "A implies B. It is the case that B, therefore A." The statement that all A are B does not imply that all B are A. We aren't told whether or not all hairy animals are mammals, so the premises don't allow us to conclude anything definite about this animal.

7 Infinite Financing

THE PROBLEM:

Many investment opportunities pay off only in the long run, and depend sensitively on how you manage your money along the way. Even a very good deal can be squandered by imprudent management. This exercise will teach you that, even over the infinitely long haul, it's the little things that kill you. Suppose I offer you the following sweetheart deal: I vow to pay you $10 every day from now till eternity, provided only that you give me back one dollar per day. That is, every day of a presumed infinite future, I will give you a stack of ten $1 bills, on the condition that each day your return $1 to me. Each day you are to place the new stack on top of your accumulated stack, and you must pay me back from this stack. Here is the question: will it matter at the end of time, when all is said and done, whether all along you have been paying me back each day from the top of your pile or from the bottom?

THE METHOD:

It is hard to see how this deal could go wrong for you, but, surprisingly, it makes all the difference in the end whether you pay me back regularly each day from the bottom or from the top. It is in your eternal best interest to pay me from the top, and not from the bottom. To see why, first consider the following hints. You may be able to come to the same conclusion on your own.

One Off the Top Daily

If you pay me back from the top, and keep on putting new stacks of bills on top, the amount you retain will grow each day. More important still, each day you pay me from among the bills I gave you that day; all the rest stay in the stack (till spent).

One From the Bottom Each Day

If you pay me back each day from the bottom, and continue as required to stack bills on the top, then after 10 days you will have paid back all the bills I gave you on day one. After 20 days, you will have returned all the bills I gave you on the first two days. On the nth day, I will have given you $10n$ bills; but I will have obtained all those bills back by the $100n^{th}$ day.

THE SOLUTION:

One Off the Top Daily

If you pay me each day from the top, then you will never return the rest of the dollars you gained from me that day. On day n, after reimbursing me, you will have 9n dollars remaining, and these you will never have to return to me, since each day you will only return one of the bills I gave you that day.

One From the Bottom Each Day

On the other hand, if you pay from the bottom, while still stacking your daily gift on top as required, you will eventually pay back every dollar I give you. This is easy to see. Simply number the bills from the bottom up. On the first day, you will return bill number one. On day 2 you return bill number two to me. On day n you will pay me back bill n. But if you pay me bill n on day n, you will have to pay me bill n+1 on day n+1. So, by mathematical induction, you will pay me back bill n for every n. That is, you pay them all back.

There is some good news, even for those foolish enough to pay from the bottom. Saving in the long run is impossible for you, but that doesn't mean that spending in the short run need be curtailed. If you try to save, in the end you will have to pay it all back, by the above argument; but in the meantime, saving works quite well.

Notice that, assuming you start by saving first to finance later splurging, your stack will increase daily by $9, just as it does in the pay-off-the-top scenario. Thus, under either payback plan, if all money but your daily $1 fee to me is saved and not spent, your stack will get larger and larger, since a net $9 income would accrue daily regardless of how I am paid.

Now notice that, once you have saved sufficient to go on a proper shopping binge, there is no reason, in either situation, to hold onto this money. However you pay your daily $1 fee, you are perfectly entitled when you like to dip into whatever savings have accumulated and spend them as you like. Indeed, there is no reason not to spend, as you can always pay tomorrow's dues with tomorrow's gains. If you pay from the top, however, you are able to spend freely of the surplus, and whatever remains will be with you in eternity. Those, however, who lack infinite foresight and are so unwise as to pay from the bottom are not so fortunate. They may spend their savings just as freely as in the other case; but should they try to build up their stack for their eternal retirement, they will be disappointed, for I will get every dollar they retain (eventually).

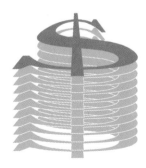

AND AND OR AND NOT

Propositional Logic

Let P, Q, R, etc. stand for propositions. Propositions may be either true or false. (True and false are called "truth values.")

We can build more and more complex propositions from these by means of connecting words such as "not," "and," "or," and "if–then." Such words play the role of *logical connectives*. We find that the truth or falsity of the more complex sentences depends wholly on the truth or falsity of their component propositions. This *truth-functionality* can be shown by introducing certain symbols and tables.

We can let ¬ stand for logical negation; so ¬P is read "not P" or "it is not the case that P." Similarly, we can introduce the symbol ∧ for "and" (logical conjunction), and another symbol ∨ standing for "or" (logical disjunction). Then (P ∧ Q) is read "P and Q," while (P ∨ Q) is read "P or Q." (We leave "if–then" propositions to subsequent pages.)

These logical relationships can be illustrated in truth tables.

How to Read a Truth Table

Each row of the truth table represents a possible situation or, as philosophers say, a possible world. The truth values in the white cells of one row determine the truth values in all the other cells of that row. In Table 1, row 1 reads: if P is true, ¬P is false. In Table 2, row 2 concerns the situation in which P is true and Q is false. Reading row 2 across the whole of Table 2, we have: if P is true and Q is false, then (P ∨ Q) is correct, but (P ∧ Q) is false. In other words, it is true that P or Q, but it is not true that P *and* Q.

We assumed P could be either true or false, so we find that the leftmost column has two rows reflecting each possibility. In the second column, we see that ¬P always has the opposite truth value to P.

Table 1

P	¬Q
T	**F**
F	**T**

↑

If we know the status of P, we can determine the status of ¬P.

The other logical connectives link two propositions, so we need four rows in the truth table, to reflect the fact that each of two component propositions can take either truth value. We need four rows because we assume that ultimately P, Q, and any additional propositions are independent of each other. If P and Q are independent, and each can be either true

Table 2

P	Q		P ∨ Q			P ∧ Q	
T	T	T	**T**	T	T	**T**	T
T	F	T	**T**	F	T	**F**	F
F	T	F	**T**	T	F	**F**	T
F	F	F	**F**	F	F	**F**	F

↑ ↑

or false, then there are four possible combinations in total, each of which is given by one row of the truth table. (The shaded columns in the table below give all four combinations.)

Truth Table Semantics

We now have an alphabet of propositions, P, Q, R, etc., and a suite of logical connectives (¬ ∧ ∨ and later →). Using only these symbols, together with precise rules of grammar, we could express well-formed sentences of any length whatsoever. Due to the truth-functionality of the logical connectives, the truth value of the longer sentence will always be a function of the truth values of its shorter components.

The meaning of logical connectives is given by their truth tables. Truth tables *define* the logical connectives. (P ∨ Q)

is true only when either P or Q is true. The only condition under which this sentence is not true is the fourth row of the table, in which P and Q are both false. In all other rows, the disjunction (P ∨ Q) is true, because at least one of its component disjunctions is true in each row. (P ∧ Q) is true only when both P and Q are true. Only the top row of the truth table represents such a case.

For any well-formed sentence (however long) we shall be able to construct its truth table, and thus determine the rows (possible situations) in which it is true. Truth tables lay out the exact conditions (rows) in which propositions are true. But the truth conditions of a proposition are its *meaning* (a proposition means what it says is true). Truth tables are a *semantics*, a theory of meaning, for propositional logic.

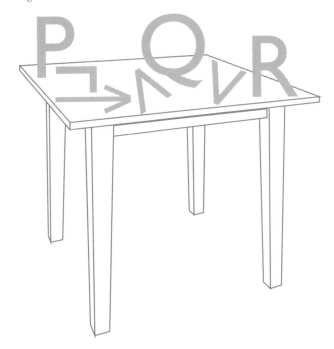

ON CONDITIONS AND CONDITIONALS

The Logic of If–Then

Sometimes, we want to assert propositions conditionally rather than outright. That is, we want to say that one is a condition of the other. You can't win unless you buy a ticket. You get 50% off if you buy today.

In propositional logic, an arrow → stands for the conditional connective. So (P → Q) can be read "if P, then Q." The table below gives some terminology related to conditional connectives.

(P → Q) can be rendered into English in other ways. One can say that Q is a necessary condition of P, or that P is sufficient for Q. It may not seem so, but (P → Q) can also be read as "P *only if* Q." If (P → Q), then if Q is not true, then

neither is P. As an exercise, prove that (¬Q → ¬P) is *logically equivalent* to (P → Q); that is, show they have the same truth table.

Conditional sentences are important in logic and philosophy because, as mentioned before, all arguments have an if–then structure. The antecedent is the conjunction of all the premises, and the consequent is the conclusion. In a deductively valid argument, the set of premises is a sufficient condition of the conclusion. The conclusion of a valid argument *follows of necessity* from the premises. (Notice that *following necessarily* is very different from *being necessary* all by itself; see pp. 94–95).

	(P → Q)	
If	P, then	Q
	antecedent	consequent
	sufficient condition	necessary condition
	e.g. premise set	conclusion

Table 3

P	Q		P → Q	
T	T	T	**T**	T
T	F	T	**F**	F
F	T	F	**T**	T
F	F	F	**T**	F

↑

How to Read This Table

Recall: each row represents a possible world. The truth values in the gray cells on the left determine the truth values in all the other cells of the same row. Notice that (P > Q) is false in only one situation (row 2). It is granted to be true whenever P is false, and also if Q is true. This weak interpretation of "if–then" is called the Philonian Conditional, after Philo of Megara, ca. 300 BCE.

We recognize many different species of necessity, and tolerate various degrees of sufficiency, depending on context. Consequently the semantics of if–then sentences in English is highly complex. In propositional logic, all such problems are averted by stipulating the meaning shown in the Truth Table at the bottom of the opposite page for →.

(Can you construct a sentence [using only, P, Q, ∨, and ¬] that has the same truth table as P → Q? Such a sentence exists; it shows that → is a redundant symbol.)

Table 3 *defines* the logical connective, →. As row 4 shows, this is a very weak definition. Not much can be said in favor of this meaning as an interpretation of ordinary language if–then sentences, but no other four-row truth table defines a workable conditional connective. It sets a kind of minimal standard of "iffiness."

Validity Revisited

Recall that all arguments have an if–then structure. So every argument has its *associated conditional.* If an argument is valid, its premises are sufficient for the conclusion. Their truth would ensure that of the conclusion. So argument validity is just the necessary truth of a conditional

sentence. *The validity of an argument consists in the logical truth of its associated conditional.*

In truth-table semantics, necessary truth means *true in every row.* Thanks to the truth-functionality of the logical connectives, truth tables turn out to be a method for testing the validity of any argument couched in propositional logic. The procedure is clear: Simply formulate the associated conditional and draw up its truth table. If the associated conditional (expressed as a long → sentence) turns up true in every row, then the argument is valid. Otherwise, it is invalid.

The existence of such a sure-fire method is remarkable in its generality. It applies in principle no matter how many premises there are, and no matter how long each one is. The truth-functionality of the connectives means we will be able in principle to construct a table, and complete it. The downside is that not all arguments can be expressed in propositional logic, nor interpreted by truth-table semantics. Next we go beyond this logic by pushing the analysis further, into the guts of propositions P and Q, hitherto assumed to be ultimately atomic. For that we need a more expressive notation: quantifier logic.

Argument	Associated Conditional
Premise-1 Premise-2 … Premise-n Conclusion	(Premise-1 ∧ Premise-2 ∧ … ∧ Premise-n) → Conclusion

Ludwig Wittgenstein

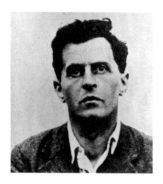

There are two Wittgensteins, early and late. Or perhaps three, if you include the view that no such bifurcation is legitimate. Here the focus is on his early book, *Tractatus Logico-Philosophicus*, which was written during World War I, in which he served for a time as a soldier before being imprisoned in 1918. The manuscript was smuggled out of prison to leading logicians, but only published with difficulty after the war in 1921.

Wittgenstein came from a highly musical family; he was a talented clarinetist and an accomplished whistler. He was fascinated by machines his entire life. His early interest in physics drove him first to engineering, where he worked on kites, jet engines, and propellers in the early days of aviation. But he soon became painfully preoccupied with problems of logic and the philosophy of mathematics. He came to know Frege (see pp. 146–147) and the pacifist Bertrand Russell before World War I, but he volunteered for service, which by some accounts was an expression of his suicidal feelings (another streak in the illustrious Wittgenstein family).

The *Tractatus*: A Disposable Ladder

The *Tractatus* consists of seven numbered propositions, to which various levels of numbered comments are attached. Extending Frege's notion of truth-functions, and critiquing Russell's monstrous Theory of Ramified Types, Wittgenstein created and introduced truth tables for the very first time. The book proceeds from an understated metaphysics of fact, through a consummate analysis of the elements of logic, toward a mysterious and even poetic silence. Nothing had ever been written like it before.

The seven major propositions are these:

1. The world is all that is the case.
2. What is the case—a fact—is the existence of states of affairs.
3. A logical picture of a fact is a thought.
4. A thought is a proposition with a sense.
5. A proposition is a truth-function of elementary propositions.
6. The general form of a truth-function is: $[p, \zeta, N(\zeta)]$. This is the general form of the proposition.
7. Whereof one cannot speak, thereof one must be silent.

Only proposition 6 is totally opaque. But elsewhere Wittgenstein puts it in very simple language: "The general form of a proposition is: this is how things stand." Put more simply still: *such are so.*

The formula in 6 cannot be briefly explained. Suffice it to say that it offers a procedure for building up all propositions from elementary propositions, much the same way that the truth tables of complex propositions are constructed from truth tables of simpler ones. Wittgenstein considered it redundant to use so many symbols (¬∨∧→) when it was known that one would do. The N in proposition 6 is like ¬ except that like the other connectives, it connects two propositions, P, Q, etc. Think of it as iterated joint denial. You can obtain all the truth tables with this one connective (see pp. 136–137).

Philosophy *Tractatus*-Style

The rest of the book contains many pregnant propositions, all comments on earlier propositions. Some of these are given below. Wittgenstein came to a skeptical conclusion about causal necessity, reminiscent of Hume's critical views.

"We cannot infer the events of the future from those of the present. The belief in the cause nexus is superstition."

"There is no compulsion making one thing happen because another has happened. The only necessity that exists is logical necessity."

At times, the *Tractatus* waxes mystical:

"*The limits of my language* mean the limits of my world."

"The world and life are one."

"I am my world. (The microcosm.)"

"It is not how things are in the world that is mystical, but that it exists."

At other times, Wittgenstein seems to deflate expectations:

"The propositions of logic are all tautologies."

"Hence there can *never* be surprises in logic."

"*The riddle* does not exist."

Arguably, this anti-surprise agenda is meant to continue Frege's war against the Kantian idea of the synthetic *a priori*. When Wittgenstein could not solve problems, he would dissolve them:

"Most of the propositions and questions to be found in philosophical works are not false but nonsensical ... And it is not surprising that the deepest problems are in fact not problems at all."

Later, he would write that:

"Philosophical problems arise when language goes on holiday."

But even in the *Tractatus* Wittgenstein held that "All philosophy is a 'critique of language'." He demanded clarity where it was possible, and silence everywhere else:

"Everything that can be thought at all can be thought clearly. Everything that can be put into words can be put clearly."

"What *can* be shown, *cannot* be said."

QUANTIFIER LOGIC

Quantifiers are words like "all," "some," and "none." They have played an important part in logic, both in ancient times and in more recent developments. We examine some of their peculiarities here.

The logic of Aristotle depends on his understanding of the meaning of quantifier words. Aristotle distinguished affirmative and negative propositions, on the one hand, and universal versus particular propositions on the other. That makes four different kinds, which exhibit complex and interesting logical relations to one another.

Aristotle founded his theory of syllogism on these relations, which are represented in his Square of Opposition.

Here are some examples of these kinds of propositions:

A: All idlers are failures.
E: No idlers are failures.
I: Some idlers are failures.
O: Some idlers are not failures.

A: All newspapers are propaganda.
E: No newspapers are propaganda.
I: Some newspapers are propaganda.
O: Some newspapers are not propaganda.

EXAMPLES

An example of a valid syllogism would be:

All lobsters are crustaceans
Some lobsters are delicacies
Some crustaceans are delicacies

This argument has the following *valid* form:

All L are C
Some L are D
Some C are D

Since this is valid, any argument of this form will also be valid.

Is this next syllogism valid?:

All lobsters are crustaceans
Some crustaceans are sow bugs
Some lobsters are sow bugs

Note the form:

All S are P
Some P are X
Some S are X

Hint: If this form is invalid, you should be able to find true premises and a false conclusion.

Invalid. Let L=birds, C=animals, and B= mammals. All birds are animals, and some animals are mammals, but (contrary to the conclusion, Some L are B) no birds are mammals.

ANSWERS

SQUARE OF OPPOSITION

This table captures the logical relations (what implies what) amongst these kinds of propositions. As in simple one-premise arguments, we can ask which propositions imply others. Armed with this knowledge, Aristotle built a theory of more complex arguments, called *syllogisms*.

The diagonal relationship is *direct contradiction*: to affirm one is to deny its diagonal opposite. If all ducks waddle, it is false that some do not. If there is no wine in your glass, it contradicts fact to say there is some. If there is some wine there, to say there is none is false.

Comparing propositions across the table from each other, you find contraries (top) and sub-contraries (bottom). Contraries can't both be true; sub-contraries can't both be false. Related "all" and "no" statements are contraries: they can't both be true, but they might both be false. Cynics say all politicians are liars. The naïve believe that no politicians are liars. They can't both be right. Indeed, they are both wrong: some politicians lie, others do not.

Sub-contraries are opposite: they can easily both be true (some people can read,

some can't). But they can't both be false. If it is false that some people can read, then nobody can read. But if nobody can read, then (trivially) some people cannot read. That shows that if an I-proposition is false, its sub-contrary O-proposition is true. Contrariwise, if we assume that an O-proposition (some people cannot read) is false, then everyone can read. If everyone can read, surely some people can (the related I-proposition is true).

To say that some S is P is to assume that there is at least one S. Put differently, particular statements have *existential import*. Until recent times, it was standard to assume that even universal statements had existential import. In that case, it would be false that "all unicorns have one horn," simply because there are no unicorns. If universal statements have existential import (if the set of Ss is not empty), then universal propositions imply their subaltern. That is, holding S and P constant, A-type propositions imply I-type propositions, and E-type propositions imply O-type propositions. This is only correct if one assumes that there is at least one S.

Universal Affirmative (**A**)
All S are P

A and E propositions are **contraries**: they can't both be true.

Universal Negative (**E**)
No S is P

This is called a **subaltern** relationship.

A and O directly **contradict** each other, as do I and E: If one is true, the other is false. If one is false, the other is true.

This is called a **subaltern** relationship.

Particular Affirmative (**I**)
Some S is P

I and O propositions are **sub-contraries**: they can't both be false.

Particular Negative (**O**)
Some S is not P

NESTED CIRCLES
(example of valid syllogism)

All A are B
All B are C
Therefore,
All A are C

This can be depicted so:

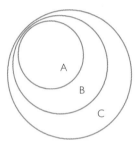

As above, A and B are classes of objects. The first premise says that A is a subset of B, so that, if we gathered all the As in a circle, and all the Bs in a circle, we would find all the As among the Bs. The circles would nest, as depicted, for everything in the circle of As is also in the circle of Bs.

This argument can also be expressed in other ways. Where ⊆ means "is a subset of," we can write the premises on one line as:

$$A \subseteq B \subseteq C$$
$$\text{Therefore, } A \subseteq C$$

Essentially the same idea can be expressed in the following way:

if x is an A, then x is a B
if x is a B, then x is a C
Therefore, if x is an A, then x is a C

The diagram of three nested circles depicts all of these arguments, despite the unique notation of each. They share what may be called *logical form*. The logical form of conditionals (if–then statements) is related to the very nature of the subset relationship, and is essential as well to what is meant in these examples by "all."

Logicians call "all" a universal quantifier. Here we see how generalization (use of a universal quantifier) involves conditionality (if–then structure), and how if–then structure can be used to define subset inclusion. We also see how logicians can use mouthfuls of large words to convey very simple ideas.

Modern logic distinguished itself from ancient and medieval logic by new insights into quantification. This stems in part from the inadequacy of attempts to unravel such complex quantificational structures as these:

•   A sucker is born every minute.
•   No net will catch all fish.
•   No fish will escape every net.
•   For every moment in time there is a later moment in time.

These can all be expressed in modern quantificational logic, but none lend themselves to an analysis based on Aristotle's Square of Opposition. Consider the sentences:

•   Everything fades.
•   Something matters.

Let's introduce new symbols ∀ and ∃ to help express these:

∀x (Fx)   For all x, x fades.
∃x (Mx)   There is an x such that x matters.

Negating these sentences has an interesting result. If it is false that everything fades, then clearly some things don't fade. In other words, ¬ ∀x (Fx) means the same thing as ∃x (¬ Fx). Similarly, if it is false that something matters, then nothing matters. Put differently, everything matters not: ¬ ∃x (Mx) is logically equivalent to ∀x (¬ Mx).

We can now convert the Square of Opposition into modern quantificational terms. By piling up quantifiers, we can now analyze the above statements as shown in the table, top right.

These examples are relatively simple. But, as we shall see, their complexity suffices to express certain major logical results, such as Gödel's theorem (see pp. 152–153).

Take the example from the opposite page that asserts that future time will go on forever. The expression ∀x∃y (x < y) can only be true in infinite domains. It says in effect that for every number, there is a higher number. From this it follows that there is no highest number.

A slight variation deals with the relationship, *being between*. Let's write Byxz for "x lies between y and z." (Also, we assume Byxz is only true when y, x, and z are all distinct.) Then we can express the infinite divisibility of space by the following formula:

∀y ∀z ∃x (Byxz).

In short, between any two points there is a third.

Universal Affirmative (A) ∀x(Sx → Px) All S are P	Universal Negative (E) ∀x(Sx → ¬ Px) No S is P
Particular Affirmative (I) ∃x(Sx ∧ Px) Some S is P	Particular Negative (O) ∃x(Sx ∧ ¬ Px) Some S is not P

A sucker is born every minute.	∀t∃x (x is a sucker ∧ x is born at time t)
Some net will catch every fish.	∃n ∀f (n catches f)
No net will catch all fish.	¬ ∃n ∀f (n catches f) Equivalently: ∀n∃f (f is not caught by n)
No fish will escape every net.	¬ ∃f ∀n (f escapes n) Equivalently: ∀f ∃n (n catches f)
For every moment in time there is a later moment in time.	∀x∃y (y is later than x) More briefly still: ∀x∃y (x < y)

Gottlob Frege

Frege was indisputably the greatest logician since Aristotle. From his head, fully formed like Athena from the brow of Zeus, emerge: modern quantificational logic (first and second order); an analysis of the inner structure of propositions modeled on mathematic functions (rather than grammar); a deductive theory of series and numbers based on logic alone (contrary to virtually everyone from Aristotle to Kant); a system of symbolic notation, with explicit rules of inference based on form or syntax, not on content or meaning.

Frege toiled in relative obscurity, wrote books that look like wallpaper, but he pointed later analytic philosophers in wholly new directions. This is especially so as regards the study of reference, meaning, function, and truth. Perhaps one of his most striking views is the idea that all true sentences refer to the same thing (namely, The True), while all false sentences refer to The False, an insensible object in Frege's ontology.

Frege invented a notation for logic which he called his *Begriffschrift*, literally Concept-Script, but also "ideography" or Idea-notation. Free from the vagueness and coloration of everyday language, Frege symbolized not only the logical connectives, but also logical quantification. His use of quantifiers went well beyond reformulating the Square of Opposition; for instance, by having multiple quantifiers in one formula. As mentioned earlier, this implies that the predicate is relational (like < or "less than" for instance), and allowed Frege to formulate propositions that could only be true of infinite series.

Frege's analysis of mathematical sequence grew from this, and he was able (in so-called "second-order" logic) explicitly to define the very concept of the natural number. This and his other efforts persuaded him that all of mathematics was pure logic. This is Frege's *logicism*. Later, Bertrand Russell read Frege and was converted to the new doctrine, which he attempted to establish in his own way.

Frege was one of the few mathematicians who embraced and admired Cantor's startling results (see pp. 164–165). The new theories of infinity too were just part of logic. He gave Hume credit for Hume's Principle, and he recognized Dedekind's principle as well. (This principle defines a set as infinite provided it is equal in size or cardinality to a proper subset of itself; see pp. 160–161.)

Frege is also responsible for inventing so-called second-order logic. That means he allowed quantifiers to reach into the P, not just the x. This small allowance in the definition of what an acceptable symbolic sentence is has profound implications. In the chart opposite, we give a few examples from common English, followed by expressions of major metaphysical principles we can now symbolize thanks to Frege.

Some critics admire only one another.	$\exists C(\exists x Cx \land \forall x \forall y(Cx \land x$ admires $y \to Cy \land y \neq x))$. **Read:** There are critics who, if they admire anyone, they admire critics other than themselves.
Some computers communicate only to one another.	Similar: substitute "x communicates with y."
There are some pitchers each of whom has beaned at least one of the others.	$\exists P \exists x [Px \land \forall y(Px \to \exists y(x$ beaned $y \land Py \land y \neq x))]$
One of these things is different from the others; some of these things are similar (to paraphrase a children's song from *Sesame Street*).	$\exists S\ \exists D\ \exists x(Sx \land \neg Dx \land \forall y(Sy \land y \neq x \to Dy))$ **Read:** At least one of these things lacks a property that all the others have. This says both less and more than the ditty. This asserts that there's *at least* one, the song *exactly* one. The song is ambiguous between the sore thumb lacking something the others share (they are all fingers) and having something they all lack (pain).
	The critics example is attributed to Peter Geatch and David Kaplan. The pitchers example and the formulas expressing them are taken from Boolos (1984).

Next there follow other second-order statements of philosophical importance:

What does not differ, cannot be different. There is no distinction without a difference.	$\forall P\ (Px \leftrightarrow Py) \to x = y$ **Read:** If x and y share all the same properties, they are identical. This principle is sometimes called the Identity of Indiscernibles, and is sometimes thought to follow from the Principle of Sufficient Reason (nothing happens without a cause or reason).
Identical objects share all the same properties. A possible application: If the murderer is tall, no one short committed the crime.	$x = y \to \forall P\ (Px \leftrightarrow Py)$ **Read:** If x and y are the same, what is true of one is true of the other. This principle is called *Indiscernibility of Identicals.* A rose by any other name would smell as sweet.

LIAR, LIAR! Part 1

Suppose someone says to you: "What I am now saying is false!" Is this person speaking the truth?

Epimenides the Cretan claims that Cretans always lie. Was he lying? If he spoke truly, then, being a Cretan, he is lying. But no one can lie by speaking the truth. So he was not lying and he was not speaking truly.

Suppose a person you have never met comes to you and says: "You will never know that what I am telling you is true." You never see or hear of this person again. Then what was said is true, but you could never know it, or it would be false.

TRUE OR NOT?

"This sentence is true."

Is the previous sentence true? There is no paradox here, but there is endless futility. To find out if the sentence is true, we look at what it is about. We find it is about itself. It will be true about itself if what it says about itself is actually the case. In other words, it will be true if it is true.

But that does not move us any closer to settling the matter at all. Neither does the opposite assumption, that it is false. If it is false, what it says about itself is not true. But it says it's true. So if it is false, it is not true. But this is as empty as it sounds, being true of any sentence at all. Again we are getting nowhere. We can keep going nowhere endlessly. As a sentence, it is semantically groundless. It is not a paradox, but merely vacuous.

It is said that we don't know what we don't know. This sounds like a tautology, but in fact it is a deep truth that invites the expansion of our intellectual horizons. But try this sentence: "We cannot refer to what we cannot refer to." This too seems like a tautology, but in fact it is impossible. If it were true, we could not refer to what it is about. We can talk about what we don't know, but we cannot talk about anything to which we cannot refer. But then what, after all, is that sentence about?

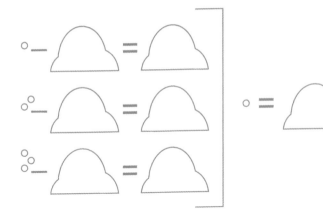

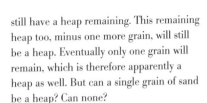

1. Paying Protagoras

Euathlus studied law (or how to argue successfully in court) under Protagoras. Protagoras was so confident of his teaching that he made this guarantee: Euathlus would only have to pay the exorbitant fees Protagoras charged if he won his first case. Euathlus completed his studies, but never practiced. At length Protagoras sued him for payment. Protagoras argued that, if Euathlus won the case, he would have to pay by virtue of their agreement. If he lost, he would have to pay by virtue of having lost. Either way, he would have to pay.

But Euathlus had learned well from the master. He argued that, if he won the case, he would not have to pay in virtue of having won. And if he lost, he would not have to pay in virtue of their agreement.

2. Paradox of the Heap

If you have a heap of sand and remove one grain, you still have a heap. A heap is a lot, so one grain won't be missed; there will still be a lot. In general, a heap minus a grain is still a heap. Applying this rule once more, we remove another grain, but

still have a heap remaining. This remaining heap too, minus one more grain, will still be a heap. Eventually only one grain will remain, which is therefore apparently a heap as well. But can a single grain of sand be a heap? Can none?

3. Surprise Examination Paradox

A teacher announces that there will be a surprise exam on an unspecified day next week. A student reasons that it cannot occur on Friday, since if Thursday passed with no exam, it would be evident that the exam would be Friday, and the surprise would be lost. Friday is ruled out, so it must happen on one of the other days of next week. But it can't happen on Thursday, since if Wednesday came and went with no exam, one would know it would have to be Thursday, again ruining the surprise. Likewise one can successively rule out Wednesday, Tuesday, and Monday. So the student announces that there will be no surprise exam in the next week (to the surprise of everyone).

LIAR, LIAR! Part 2

4. The Berry Paradox

Consider "the least integer not nameable in fewer than nineteen syllables." Clearly some integers can be named with fewer than nineteen syllables. 19 can be named in two: nine-teen. Generally speaking, as integers get larger and larger, one will require more and more syllables to name them. (There are only so many syllables in English, and we have to start combining them sooner or later.)

The problem is that "the least integer not nameable in fewer than nineteen syllables" can be defined in eighteen syllables. Which eighteen syllables? These: "the least integer not nameable in fewer than nineteen syllables."

5. A Paradox From Zeno of Elea

Consider two distinct points A and B. Any two points determine a line, so imagine the line that passes continuously between them. Between any two points there is a third, call it C. A and C are obviously distinct, so (by the same principle) there

must be yet another between them, call it D. Again A and D are two distinct points, so now a fifth must lie between them. We can continue in like manner without end. Therefore, *between any two points there are infinitely many points.*

This is called the *infinite divisibility* of space. Since A and B are arbitrary, it means that there are infinitely many points between any two points, however near or far. There are even infinitely many points between your thumb and index finger, however close together you may hold them, provided only that they are not touching.

Now imagine an arrow that flies from A to B. Imagine that A is your present location, where you have your arrow slung and ready. B is the bullseye on a target across a field. For the arrow to reach its target, it must fly from point A to point B. Between any two points there are infinitely many points. So the arrow must pass through infinitely many points as it flies from A to B.

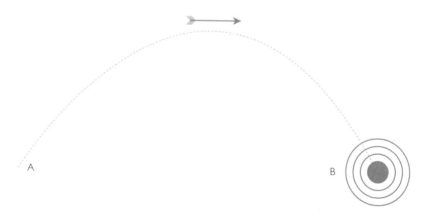

A

B

Philosophy: Adventures in Thought and Reasoning

The arrow flies so fast, we say it arrives in no time. But that is not literally true. Clearly it takes some finite amount of time to reach the target. How much time does it spend at each point? (We can ask about the average time spent at each point, but let's assume the arrow has a constant speed, and so spends the same amount of time at each point.)

There seem to be only three options, setting up a triple disjunctive syllogism (the kind familiar to dogs, as we saw earlier). Either the (average) time spent at each point is zero, or it is finite, or it is infinite.

It would be absurd to suppose that an infinite time passed at each point of the arrow's flight, since then the arrow would never leave the bow, let alone arrive as quickly as it does.

Rather, the average time spent at each of the points would seem to be finite, albeit very brief. And yet any finite number, however minuscule, multiplied by infinity equals infinity. Any finite duration is too long, since there are infinitely many points, and the arrow must spend that amount of time at each of them. Infinitely many nanoseconds is still forever. In language we explain later, $\frac{1}{n} \times \aleph_0 = \aleph_0$ (any fraction times infinity is infinite).

The only solution remaining is that the arrow spends zero time (no time) at each point in its flight.

In zero time, there is zero motion. Zero motion is rest, so the arrow is at rest at every moment of its flight. And anyway, how can infinitely many zeros add up to exactly the time it takes the arrow to complete its flight?

Zeno's own conclusion was that motion was impossible; it had to be an illusion. This is the one philosophical position that can be refuted by a hand-waving argument. But if we dislike the conclusion, where is the error made? Can you think of an alternative?

EXERCISES

Yes or No?
Have you stopped masturbating in public? (If yes, congratulations! If no, perhaps you should seek help!)

True or False?
This sentence is false.
This sentence is true.

The next sentence is false.
The previous sentence is true.

Other Questions
(Cognitive Illusions)

1. You are participating in a race. You overtake the second person. What position are you in?
2. If you overtake the last person in the race, then you are…?
3. Mary's father has five daughters: The first four are called: Nana, Nene, Nini, and Nono. What is the name of the fifth daughter?

Kurt Gödel

We are all familiar with arithmetic, with addition and multiplication of the natural numbers (zero and all the positive integers). It has been axiomatized, in the sense that a manageable set of sentences written in the language of arithmetic is selected, from which it is hoped to validly deduce all and only the truths of arithmetic. Each possible axiom set determines a set of theorems, that is, the set of statements of arithmetic that can be validly deduced by taking just those axioms as assumptions. Theoremhood is always relative to an axiom set, just as a conclusion is only valid relative to a premise set.

We can now ask the question, for any given axiomatization of arithmetic, whether or not the set of theorems provable from those axioms coincides exactly with the set of all arithmetical truths. Think of axiomatization as a net, and provability as the catch we get by casting the net. All the fish in the sea are the truths of arithmetic. We want no by-catch, so that no falsehoods get taken up in our net. (Our proofs must be deductively valid.) But we want all the fish, too. Getting all the fish is called completeness.

Gödel showed that no net will catch all fish. All axiomatizations of arithmetic are incomplete. He did not show that some truths can never be proved, any more than he proved the existence of fish that can never be caught. Rather, he showed that for every net cast there will be some fish that get away. These will be truths unprovable relative to that system. Other nets, other castings, may well catch them; but from these castings, too, yet other fish will escape. It will not help to knit all nets together, and make one great casting, for even then the ingenious Gödel will not only prove that some fish get away—he will catch one and show it to you!

Gödel is acclaimed as the greatest logician of the 20th century. A precocious and sickly boy, he proved remarkable and revolutionary theorems in mathematical logic while yet a young man. Born of German ancestry in Moravia, he first became an Austrian (he had glancing contact with the positivist Vienna Circle of philosophers), then an American. Einstein himself attended his oath of allegiance. Gödel spent the last years of his life concerned with broad philosophical issues such as the immateriality of mind, the reality of time, and the existence of an afterlife.

Undecidable Arithmetic

Gödel was the first to demonstrate the existence of undecidable propositions in mathematics. In a way, this is an assurance that mathematical genius is a renewable resource, and we shall never exhaust possible creative new ways to discover mathematical truth.

It is easy to give a mechanical procedure by which to enumerate all statements of arithmetic, true or false (they are, after all, all finite statements in a finitary language). It is relatively straightforward to give a mechanical procedure generating all theorems (that is, only statements provable from a given axiom set); for a proof is just a finite string of finite sentences, each of which is an axiom or follows by a valid rule from earlier sentences in the list. It is impossible, however, to give effective procedures to specify all and only those statements (written in the language of arithmetic) that happen to be true. Although the set of arithmetical truths is a subset of the set of arithmetical statements, the subset is far harder to specify than the whole. It contains a whole lot more information.

The One that Got Away

Gödel's famous first incompleteness theorem has several forms, but none is more delightful than the story form told by Raymond Smullyan. The story offers a flavor of the fish that gets away from a given casting, but which Gödel's methods manage to catch after all. Suppose there is an island inhabited by knights and knaves. Knights always tell the truth (they are like sound proofs). Knaves always lie. The trouble is, one cannot tell a knight from a knave. Now suppose an islander comes up and says to you: "You will never know that I am a knight." If you ever manage to prove he is a knight, what he says will be false (so he could not, after all, be a knight). But if he is a knave, surely you will never know he is a knight, simply because he isn't one. So what he said is true, which shows he is no knave. (It may not prove it in the system.)

Gödel provides an effective procedure by which to convert any axiomatization of arithmetic into a statement of arithmetic not provable in that system. "This statement is not arithmetically provable" is an illustration in English. If it were arithmetically provable, then it would not be arithmetically provable. So it is not arithmetically provable, which means it's true, since that, after all, is what it says. We can know the statement to be true, but only by so discussing it outside of the system of arithmetic.

Gödel also proved that mathematics will never be able to prove its own consistency. Of course, few mathematicians believe mathematics is inconsistent; and, if it is all true, then it is clearly consistent. But this knowledge (if it is such) is not provable mathematically.

Gödel spent the last decades of his life in the rarified atmosphere of the Institute for Advanced Studies at Princeton in the United States. He became a friend and daily acquaintance of Einstein, whose death in 1955 deeply moved him. Like Einstein, Gödel held a long interest in Kant's philosophy of space and time, and developed his own mathematical interpretation of Einstein's physical equations. (Einstein's field equations are the keystone of his General Theory of Relativity, which pertains to curved space.) In Gödel's interpretation, time could go backward, and even time travel could be possible.

THE SET OF NOTHING

ZERO IS NOT NOTHING: IT IS A NUMBER

The discovery of zero was a momentous event. The idea of a number for nothing provoked resistance, because to say that zero exists sounds uncomfortably like the claim that nothing exists. But even as a mere place-holder in calculation, a numeral for zero simplified arithmetical notation and the rules for calculation. Nobody worries about zero any more because it is so useful. Nothing is as useful as zero!

THE POWER SET AXIOM

A frankly indispensable axiom of set theory is the *power set* axiom. Take any set. The power set of that set is the set of all its subsets. The power set axiom says that every set has a power set.

Suppose a gardener offers you your choice of flowers from a garden. You may take as many as you like, including any one, none, or all. If there are n flowers in this garden, how many choices do you have?

Each choice is a subset of the original set of n flowers. And each distinct subset represents a choice. So the number of your choices is the number of subsets. The number of your choices is a measure of the size (or *cardinality*) of the power set.

If a set has n members, the power set has 2^n members. The power set gets its name from the exponent: 2^n (read: 2 to the power of n) means 2 multiplied by itself n times $2 \times 2 \times 2 \times \ldots \times 2$ (n times). Since, for all finite n, $n < 2^n$, the power set is always larger than the original set. Finite sets always have fewer members than they have subsets.

The power set axiom is very powerful. It greatly expands the number of things that might be thought to exist. Say the garden had a mere ten flowers. Once we grant the existence of a set of these ten flowers, the power set axiom will increase our ontological commitments by over 1000 new entities ($2^{10} = 1024$). If the garden were home to only 100 flowers, the mere existence of a set containing all of them would imply, if this axiom is true, some 126 7650600228229401496703205376 = 2^{100} additional entities. With each new flower, the gardener's generosity is doubled. The matter becomes extreme, we shall see, when we admit the axiom of infinity. How many choices would you have if the garden contained infinitely many flowers?

The power set axiom is on a collision course with Occam's Razor (see p. 92), a metaphysical principle that prohibits the assumption of more entities than necessary.

The Empty Set Is Not Nothing: It Is a Set with Nothing in It

In a branch of mathematics known as *set theory*, there is a creature similar to zero known as the empty set, a set that contains precisely no elements. It is so similar to zero, that zero can be defined in set theory as the empty set. (It is possible to "do arithmetic" in set theory, and to code numbers, calculation rules, even proofs, entirely in terms of sets; set theory *includes* arithmetic.)

The empty set is a peculiar beast. On first hearing, it too may provoke a resistance. But the empty set is not nothing. It only contains nothing. To say that the empty set exists is not to say that nothing exists, or even to say that there are zero things. It is to say that there is something with nothing in it.

The empty set has been compared to an empty box. The problem with this image is that sets are defined by their members. Sets are like bunches of things: if you have a different bunch, you have a different set (or at least the *makings* of a new set).

Sets are identified and distinguished by the members they contain. Nothing else matters. But the empty set contains nothing. So it is more like the emptiness of the box than like the box with nothing in it. After all, sets are not really boxes. But the empty set is really empty.

The fact is strange, but it is not a paradox. Or rather, if it is a paradox, it is a *veridical paradox*: it strikes one as wrong or counterintuitive, but it is true after all. It fits the category of "strange but true." The appearance of paradox is removed by realizing that the two statements have distinct logical form:

Nothing exists.
There is something that contains nothing.

We can use quantifier logic to express this difference.

It is difficult to express "nothing exists" in quantificational terms, but this is one attempt:

$$\neg\, \exists\, P\ \exists x Px$$

This is more like saying that nothing has any properties. A more standard expression would be:

$$\neg \exists x\ (x{=}x)$$
or equivalently: $\forall x\ (x{\neq}x)$

The assumption here is that anything that exists must be identical to itself. So if nothing is identical with itself, nothing exists at all. (Joke: Only Nothing lacks self identity.) The simplest way to express "nothing exists" might be $\neg \exists x$, but that expression is incomplete, so it asserts nothing (which is very different from asserting that nothing exists). On the other hand, asserting the existence of the empty set is relatively easy. What we want to say is that there is a set with nothing in it. If we can use $\in$ to stand for the set-membership relationship, we have:

$$\exists y \forall x (x \notin y)$$

We can say that the empty set is also distinguished by its membership: it is the only set without members. The empty set is like a club that is so exclusive it doesn't have anyone as a member. It is distinguished precisely by its having no members.

THE SET OF EVERYTHING

The power set axiom does not apply to gardens, only to sets. So the question arises: which sets are there? Originally, it seemed that, if there could be a set with nothing in it, there could be a set with everything in it, a set of everything. This universal set has everything at all as a member. It is not the universe (the garden is not a set), but everything in the universe is a member of this set. Can such a set exist?

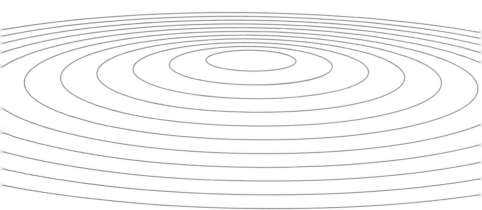

This universal set is paradoxical in the extreme. If it exists, it is clearly a member of itself (since it includes everything as a member). Furthermore, if the power set axiom is true, the power set of the universal set must also exist: so the universal set has its own power set as a member. Indeed, every subset of the universal set must also exist: all of its subsets are also its members.

Now there arises a certain problem. We saw earlier that the power set of a set is always larger than the set, just as there are more choices than flowers in the garden. But how can there be more subsets of things than there are things at all? The universal set contains everything, so it is presumably the biggest thing there is. What could be larger than the set of everything? Indeed, if the universal set includes as a member each and every subset of itself, then it must be at least as big as its power set. Indeed, its power set is a subset of itself, since every subset of the universal set belongs as a member to the universal set.

If you smell a rat, your nose is good. The great mathematical pioneer of the infinite, Georg Cantor, had proven that the power set of a set is always larger than the set.

In 1901, while struggling with this theorem, Bertrand Russell felt the same unease, and attempted to refute Cantor. He tried to do so by establishing a 1:1 correlation between the universal set and its power set. Using Cantor's own diagonal technique (see pp. 164–165), he was led to consider the following set:

- the set of all sets that do not contain themselves as members;
- the set y containing all and only sets x such that $x \notin x$;
- the set y such that $x \in y \leftrightarrow x \notin x$.

It is comaprable to the Grelling Paradox concerning the adjective *heterological*. A word is heterological if and only if it does not apply to itself—the word "long," for example, is heterological because it is not a long word. So is *heterological* heterological? If it applies to itself, it does not. If it does not apply to itself, it is.

The question Russell then asked was whether or not $y \in y$. Neither answer seemed possible:

$$y \in y \leftrightarrow y \notin y$$
or
If $y \in y$, then $y \notin y$.
And if $y \notin y$, then $y \in y$.

This is the famous paradox named Russell's paradox.

RUSSELL'S PARADOX

What Russell's Paradox really shows is that the universal set does not exist. Similarly, imagine a village with a barber who shaves all and only those villagers who do not shave themselves. Who shaves the barber?

If he shaves himself, he is not one of those who do not shave themselves (these are the only people he shaves).

If he does not shave himself, he qualifies to be one of those he does shave (he shaves all such).

We can likewise conclude that there is no such barber, no such village. The paradox in both cases dissolves into a *reductio ad absurdum*.

Russell's reaction was dramatic. Over the next few years he denied there were any sets at all (his so-called "no-class" theory). Since that did not solve all the problems, to rid himself of contradiction, Russell introduced so-called Ramified Type Theory, which prohibited the use of "all" to refer to absolutely everything. You could not quantify over everything, but only everything of a certain type. In reply, a great logician once said: "When I say everything, I mean everything."

Eventually Russell had to admit that, if Ramified Type Theory was logic, mathematics was not logic. Like Frege's, Russell's logicism collapsed.

PARADOXES OF INFINITY

The Cone of Democritus

As almost everyone knows from school, the area A of a circle is given by the formula $A=\pi r^2$, where r is the radius of the circle and π is pi, that peculiar irrational number 3.1415926… The formula for the volume of a cylinder is not much different: $V=\pi r^2 h$, where h is the height of the cylinder. You can think of a 3D cylinder as a stack of infinitely many 2D disks of the same radius r.

The same applies to the cone, except that the radius of the disks gets smaller and smaller as you approach the vertex of the cone, where it becomes zero. The formula for the volume of a mathematical solid in the shape of a cone: $V= \frac{1}{3} \pi r^2 h$.

This formula was discovered by the ancient Greek mathematician Democritus (5th century BCE), famous as a philosopher for developing physical atomism. Unlike the atoms of today, the atoms conceived by Democritus were indivisible constituents of material reality. Though invisible, his atoms had a tiny finite size and definite shapes, which allowed them to give rise to various sensory qualities (like sweet, red, shrill, etc.).

Mathematical Atomism

But Democritus also invented a kind of mathematical atomism, with infinitely small atoms, which he used to derive the formula for the volume of the cone.

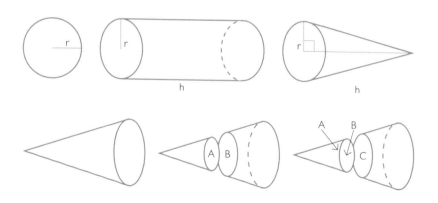

A=new base of the apex
B=new top of the bottom (called a rostrum)

This shows a supposed adjacent slice, with B now base of the apex, presumed adjacent to both A and C.

Take a pure mathematical solid cone. For convenience, lay it on its side. Now slice it *anywhere at all* along its length, parallel to the base. It is natural to think that two circular faces would be revealed, two adjacent 2D disks of which the cone is composed. Call them A and B.

Now compare areas A and B (middle figure). Initially, the only two plausible options are that A<B or that A=B.

Democritus apparently considered both answers to be problematic. And one can see why, because if A<B, then if one were to reassemble the cone, A would not fit B. Instead, if you reassembled the cone, there would now be a discontinuity in its otherwise smooth side.

On the other hand, if A=B, then any two adjacent disks must be equal. (Recall: the location of the slice was chosen arbitrarily). Clearly, if any two adjacent disks are equal, surely any three adjacent disks are equal. If the cone had been cut "one over" as it were, so that B were the base of the apex, and the disk to its immediate right formed the top of the rostrum, then A (now the inside of the bottom face of the apex) would equal B and B would equal C. Put differently, wherever you slice, there are equals all around.

But now a new trouble arises. By syllogism, if A=B=C, then A=C. It seems that if one were to slice the cone up entirely, the 2D disks would all equal their neighbors, which would also equal their neighbors, and so on. But then if you

THOUGHT EXPERIMENT

For comparison, consider the following infinite series of fractions, n/n+1:

½, ⅔, ¾, ⅘, ⅚, ⅞, ⁸⁄₉, ⁹⁄₁₀, ¹⁰⁄₁₁, …

There is no end to this series, each member of which is slightly closer to one than the preceding member. Yet no member of the series will ever equal 1. The revealed non-surface is similar to this open interval.

reassemble the equal-sized disks, you should get a cylinder, not a cone.

It seems then that neither A<B nor A=B. (And surely not B<A.) The difference between A and B must therefore be infinitely small, that is, a non-zero quantity less than any fraction 1/n. Such infinitely small quantities are known as infinitesimals. Today we know that the theory of infinitesimals is perfectly consistent (provided real number arithmetic itself is logically consistent).

But there is a problem with this argument. In space, there are no immediate neighbors, no adjacent planes. (Recall: between any two points there is a third.) In fact, if you slice a mathematical solid, only one surface is revealed. In place of the other is a finite but unbounded area.

INFINITY AND BEYOND

Galileo's Fan

Imagine a single point, V, the vertex of a two-dimensional cone (a fan).

Now imagine two parallel line segments (L and M) just long enough to reach the sides of the fan (as depicted below). L and M can be any distance apart you choose, each arbitrarily near or far from V. (For instance, M might be the distance from the sun to the nearest star, and L could be the distance between your thumb and forefinger, about to pinch.)

Now consider any straight line (shown dotted) passing through V like a ray and falling within the fan, so that it crosses both L and M.

Any ray passing through V and L will cross M at one and only one point. Any ray passing through V and M will have crossed L at one and only one point. In other words, the rays through V falling inside the fan establish a one-to-one correspondence between the points that make up L and the points that make up M. (Here we tacitly assume that line segments are made up of points.)

It follows from this 1:1 correspondence that there are the same number of points in L as in M, despite the fact that L and M have such vastly different lengths. Indeed, if the arms of the fan were extended infinitely, and one considered the infinite line between them (the top of the fan, so to speak, at infinity), then even this infinitely long line would contain no more points than exist between your thumb and forefinger, held apart however slightly. The same argument establishes a 1:1 correlation between L and an infinite line.

Galileo knew of this 1:1 correspondence, and concluded (quite in keeping with Aristotle and St. Thomas Aquinas) that human beings have no conception of infinity. The paradox is taken as irresolvable, and the human idea of infinity as incoherent. But what Galileo considered impossible is today accepted as routine. The equal number of points in lines of arbitrary length is strange, but true.

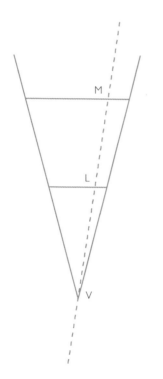

Hume's Banquet

Imagine you enter a long, narrow banquet hall, with a single rectangular table that extends into the infinite distance. As far as your eye can see, the settings look identical: a fork, a spoon, and a knife, a soup bowl and a dinner plate. A waiter informs you that the opposite end of the table has never been found, that every setting ever seen is identical, and that the table may be presumed to be infinite.

If all the settings are identical, one can prove that there are the same number of forks on the table as there are dinner plates, without ever having to count them (which is convenient, since counting would take forever). Once again, there is a 1:1 correlation between the spoons and the bowls: for each spoon, there is one bowl; for each bowl, there is one spoon. As long as one knows this, one can know there are the same number of spoons and bowls, whether or not the table is finitely long. This principle (that 1:1 correspondence proves equinumerosity) is valid for finite and infinite sets.

This principle is sometimes called Hume's Principle, after the Scottish skeptic, David Hume. Another principle at play here (that infinite sets are equal in size to partial subsets of themselves) is called Dedekind's Principle, in honor of Richard Dedekind, who first saw it, not as an absurdity, but as a (weak) definition of infinity.

PUZZLE

How many ways can you walk up a three-step staircase?

You can step on every step. You can step over all steps. Or you can step on some combination of steps. How many ways up are there?

If you figured that one out, try this. Suppose the staircase had n steps in it, where n is any finite number. You may suppose that your legs are arbitrarily long, so that reaching over all n steps is one way up (i.e., stepping on zero steps while passing over all of them counts as one way up). You can step on any combination of steps. How many ways are there up an n-step staircase?

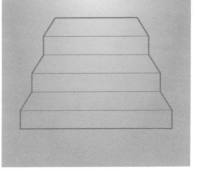

STAIRWAYS TO HEAVEN

Now consider an infinite staircase: for every step, there is a next higher step. $\forall x \exists y$ (y is one step up from x).

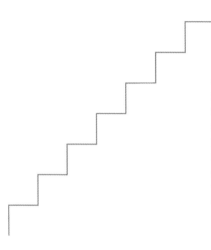

A deity sufficiently astonishing would be able to learn at an accelerating rate, so that, if it did anything once, it could do it the next time in only half as long. That granted, it will not be hard to imagine that this deity can take its first step up the staircase in half a second. The sum of the times this speedy god spends ascending to each step would look like this:

$$\frac{1}{2} + \frac{1}{4} + \frac{1}{8} + \frac{1}{16} + \frac{1}{32} + \frac{1}{64} + \frac{1}{128} + \frac{1}{256} + \ldots$$

Imagine further that each step is capable of lighting up when stepped upon. Step on it again, and the light goes off. To begin, the steps are all unlit. Now, if you walk up the steps by twos, then every other step will be lit, leaving a pattern reflecting this particular way of climbing an infinite staircase. Other ways up will leave other patterns. The question is: *Are there more patterns than steps? How many ways can you climb an infinite staircase?*

Readers who are mortal will no doubt reply: zero! Nobody can climb an infinite staircase. Only those who retain the divine spark of imagination need read on. Let us abstract away from human and physical constraints—in short, let's disregard them. Entertain an "as if" for the sake of philosophy and self-education.

This infinite sum, however, equals 1. In other words, after one second, this deity has stepped on every step and the entire staircase is lit up. In very short order, this deity surpasses the speed of light, which is physically impossible; but this only proves our being is a genuine deity, and not any physical thing.

Needless to say, this powerful being is capable of leaping up any number of steps at once. Lifting one foot only once, it can come down on any step higher than its current place. It steps over the entire staircase at one go, as easily as you transcend a three-step staircase merely by stretching up one leg.

With these few remarkable assumptions, we can see that any possible pattern of lit and unlit steps could occur, left by this deity after only one second of climbing. Now our question becomes: How many ways can a deity so endowed climb an infinite staircase? How many infinite patterns of on and off are there? How many ways can a god dance to heaven? As before, we can think of the various patterns as distinct subsets of the staircase. Each subset consists of all the lit steps in a given pattern. Since the staircase is really just the counting numbers represented in an image, we are really asking how many subsets of the counting numbers there are.

In other words, what is the size of the power set of the counting numbers? Are there more subsets of counting numbers than there are counting numbers?

Let $\aleph_0$ (pronounced *aleph-null*) stand for the number of steps in the staircase. $\aleph_0$ is an infinite cardinal number, which to say it is a measure of infinite size. $\aleph_0$ is also called *countably infinite*. The number of subsets of a countably infinite set is $2^{\aleph_0}$. It took the genius of mathematician Georg Cantor to prove that, as it happens, $\aleph_0 < 2^{\aleph_0}$. In other words, there are more patterns than steps, more subsets of counting numbers than counting numbers to begin with, more ways to dance to heaven than there are steps in a stairway to heaven. Cantor went further, generalizing this to what is known in his honor as Cantor's Theorem (see next page).

QUESTION

Consider this. How many fractions are there? That is, if a and b are counting numbers, how many rational numbers are there of the form a/b?

Before you respond, consider merely those fractions between 0 and 1, so-called proper fractions. That is, how many numbers are there of the form a/b such that $0 < a/b < 1$? Notice that all of the fractions mentioned so far are included (and many more):

.... $1/256$ ... $1/128$ ... $1/64$ ... $1/32$ ... $1/16$ ... $1/8$ ... $1/4$ ... $1/2$ ... $2/3$ ... $3/4$ ... $4/5$ ... $5/6$ ... $7/8$ ... $8/9$ ... $9/10$ ... $10/11$

1/1	1/2	1/3	1/4	1/5	...
2/1	2/2	2/3	2/4	2/5	...
3/1	3/2	3/3	3/4	3/5	...
4/1	4/2	4/3	4/4	4/5	...
5/1	5/2	5/3	5/4	5/5	...
...	...	...	...	...	...

1	1/2	1/3	1/4	1/5	...
2	1	2/3	2/4	2/5	...
3	3/2	1	3/4	3/5	...
4	2	4/3	1	4/5	...
5	5/2	5/3	5/4	1	...
...	...	...	...	...	...

In fact, you could create a table of all fractions (above top). All the fractions are here, although there are numerous duplications. For instance, we could represent the same table in another way (above). Notice that the diagonal is all 1s. Above the diagonal are all fractions less than one.

Georg Cantor

Mathematician Georg Cantor almost single-handedly created a mathematical science of infinity (set theory). He was led to it through his fundamental discovery (shared with Dedekind and others) concerning the analysis of the mathematical continuum. This wickedly difficult problem, dubbed by Leibniz the "labyrinth of the continuum," arises by a conjunction of Zeno's paradoxes and Pythagorean incommensurable magnitudes. Put simply, the question is whether a theory of the so-called real numbers (the rational and irrational numbers together) exists that exactly and completely analyzes the intuitive notion of continuity.

Mystery Resolved

The hope that a theory of *numbers* could crack the mystery of the continuum seems to have inspired Democritus, as a response to his paradoxical cone. Galileo had said that the book of Nature was written in the language of geometry. But the familiar x–y axis coordinate system (the Cartesian plane) promised to reduce geometrical forms to coordinate pairs of real numbers. The mathematical calculus that lay behind modern physics, invented by Newton and Leibniz, rested on a theory of real numbers, but such a theory was still a hope in Cantor's day. Cantor was one of the mathematicians who solved this problem. But his theory of numbers was based squarely upon his mathematics of the infinite, his set theory.

Critics were fierce. How could one mystery (infinity) explain another mystery (the continuum)? One arch-rival, a finitist professor of mathematics who opposed Cantor's bold new ideas, quipped that "God made the integers; all the rest is the work of man."

Cantor suffered mental collapse, and in fact ended his days in a sanatorium. But opinion eventually shifted, and set theory developed rapidly in the 20th century. The great mathematician David Hilbert called set theory Cantor's Paradise, for the infinite realm of mathematics it opened to mortals, declaring that we shall never be made to abandon it.

Paradox or Proof?

Interestingly, Cantor was in possession of Russell's Paradox well before Russell. But he merely considered it a proof that there is no set of everything. He even called sets "consistent multiplicities," in contrast to "inconsistent multiplicities" like absolutely everything. Indeed, Cantor recognized an *absolute infinity*, incapable of mathematical determination, greater in size even than any infinite number, in fact so multitudinous that to think of it as one is to contradict yourself.

For Cantor, Russell's Paradox was just the absurdity to which you were reduced by assuming that infinity was limited to the endless infinite numbers that he himself had discovered.

This had implications for Cantor's theory of the real numbers. The size of the set of real numbers was larger than $\aleph_0$ (aleph-null), hence uncountably infinite. Cantor hypothesized that the size of the set of real numbers was not just greater than $\aleph_0$, but actually equal to $2^{\aleph_0}$. This famous conjecture is called the *Continuum Hypothesis*. In its most general form, it turns out to be logically independent of Cantor's set theory. In short, so far, nobody knows.

DOING THE DIAGONAL

Cantor's Theorem

For every infinite size, there is a larger infinite size. More precisely, for every infinite number $\aleph$, $\aleph < 2^{\aleph}$

Cantor proved his theorem with the so-called diagonal argument. A flavor of this ingenious method can be gathered if we return to the question, how many different ways can you climb an infinite staircase? Cantor's argument is a *reductio*: that is, we get to assume that, indeed, one can enumerate all such ways, which can therefore be given in an infinite table shown here.

Each row represents one way up, if you like, one pattern left by the ascended deity. I s represent "on"s (which were stepped on) and 0s represent missed steps (off or unlit).

Our assumption is that all the patterns are in this table. But Cantor was able to construct a pattern not in this table, simply by following the diagonal and inverting the values at each step. Presented with any purported enumeration of all the patterns, Cantor showed how to construct a pattern not in that enumeration. His diagonal method, applied to the above table, results in the following pattern, which is sure to be nowhere in the above table, since it will differ from the n-th row at the n-th place.

0	I	0	I	0	...
I	0	I	0	I	...
0	0	I	0	I	...
I	0	I	0	I	...
I	I	0	I	I	...
0	0	0	I	0	...
...	...	...	...	...	...

I	I	0	I	0	...

The number of ways to ascend an infinite staircase are innumerable, that is unenumerable, in short, *uncountably infinite*. There are more ways up than steps up the staircase.

8   Hilbert's Heartbreak Hotel

THE PROBLEM:

You are traveling in a strange (and very large) city, attending the strange (and very large) Odd-Fellows Convention, only you forgot to book a room for the night. You inquire around at the convention, and it seems everyone at the convention will be staying at the same place, the Heartbreak Hotel.

Despite its name, you learn that the Heartbreak Hotel will not let you down; you are assured there will be a room for you. You suspect this is just advertising, but are authoritatively told that, though the hotel is completely full, you need only inquire at the desk and you are sure to find accommodation there for the night.

THE METHOD:

The sign above the door reads "Hilbert's Heartbreak Hotel." At the front desk you are politely greeted by a certain Prof. David Hilbert, genius mathematician as well as designer and proprietor. What he tells you may help you to solve the problem: although the hotel is indeed full, it is also infinite. More exactly, it has a countably infinite number of rooms, numbered 1, 2, 3, …. In symbols introduced earlier, the number of rooms is $\aleph_0$. Each room accommodates a single person only. You also learn that you are indeed the first of the convention to check in. Prof. Hilbert then assures you that you will indeed get a room, as will all the other convention attendees. Perplexed, you ask, "If every room is full, in which room will I stay?" "I'll put you in room number one," the unperturbed professor replies, "and have everyone currently in room number n (where n is any whole or counting number) move to room n+1. You see, everyone moves along one room, which everyone can do because there is no room with a largest number. For every room number, there is a larger room number. That is just what it means to be an infinite hotel."

Fine for you, you think, but the convention is large, and the attendees most numerous. The professor explains, "If there were only 1000 more coming tonight, I could accommodate them by a similar strategy. I would merely have the current occupant of room n move to room n+1000. There will be enough rooms, because for every n, there is a room number n+1000. That trick would leave the first 1000 rooms free for your co-conventionalists.

"But you are attending the Odd-Fellows Convention, which is a countably infinite conference. I know this because each member of the convention is assigned a unique odd number, and every odd number is assigned to some member or other. Now, since for every odd number, there is a larger odd number (just add 2), it follows that there are $\aleph_0$ odd numbers. The attendees, being equinumerous with the odd numbers, are therefore also countably infinite (by Hume's Principle, see p. 161). So I need another approach to distributing rooms to the $\aleph_0$ new guests who will arrive tonight; but I can accommodate them all, each to his own room."

The principle involved so far is this. For any finite number n,

$$n + \aleph_0 = \aleph_0$$

This is how you plus 1000 friends can be accommodated in Hilbert's Hotel, though it is already booked solid. How can the rooms be redistributed differently so that now $\aleph_0$ rooms are freed up to accommodate the $\aleph_0$ convention delegates, who have now as predicted arrive en masse in the lobby and are clamoring for their rooms? Come up with and test your own answers before reading on.

asked to move to room 2n. The current guests will then occupy all and only even-numbered rooms, leaving all the odd-numbered rooms available for the new guests. Since all the members of the convention have been assigned their own odd number, they can go into the room of the same number, which is now free. So, where $\aleph_0$ is the number of items in countably infinite set, we have

$$\aleph_0 + \aleph_0 = \aleph_0$$

The number of odd numbers is the same as the number of even numbers, but also the same as the number of counting numbers as a whole. Thus countably infinite sets are the same size as half—or even a tenth—of themselves. This is proved by reflection on the following arrangement:

1	3	5	7	9	11	15	15	...
↑↓	↑↓	↑↓	↑↓	↑↓	↑↓	↑↓	↑↓	↑↓
1	2	3	4	5	6	7	8	...
↑↓	↑↓	↑↓	↑↓	↑↓	↑↓	↑↓	↑↓	↑↓
10	20	30	40	50	60	70	80	...

THE SOLUTION:

All rooms are currently occupied. But suppose guests currently in room n are

INDEX OF PHILOSOPHERS

Empiricus, Sextus
Dates: 2nd Century–3rd Century
Nationality: Unknown
Most famous work: *Outlines of Pyrrhonism*
See page: 129

Epicurus
Dates: 341–270 BCE
Nationality: Greek
Most famous work: *Letter to Heroditus*
See pages: 68

Epimenides the Cretan
Dates: 6th Century BCE
Nationality: Greek
Most famous work: *Cretica*
See page: 148

Euathlus
Dates: 5th Century BCE
Nationality: Greek
See page: 149

Fechner, Gustav
Dates: 1801–1887
Nationality: German
Most famous work: *Elemente der Psychophysik*
See page: 107

Frege, Gottlob
Dates: 1848–1925
Nationality: German
Most famous work: *Foundations of Arithmetic*
See pages: 140–141, 146–147, 157

Freud, Sigmund
Dates: 1856–1939
Nationality: Austrian
Most famous work: *Three Essays on the Theory of Sexuality*
See page: 104

Galileo Galilei
Dates: 1564–1642
Nationality: Italian
Most famous work: *Dialogue Concerning the Two Chief World Systems*
See pages: 92, 160, 164

Gaunilo
Dates: 11th Century
Nationality: French
Most famous work: *In Defense of the Fool*
See page: 113

Gautama
see Buddha

Gettier, Edmund
Dates: b. 1927
Nationality: American
Most famous work: *Is Justified True Belief Knowledge?*
See pages: 12, 26–27

Gilligan, Carol
Dates: b. 1936
Nationality: American
Most famous work: *In a Different Voice*
See page: 70

Gödel, Kurt
Dates: 1906–1978
Nationality: Austrian American
Most famous work: First Incompleteness Theorem
See pages: 145, 152–153

Goldman, Alvin
Dates: b. 1938
Nationality: American
Most famous work: *A Causal Theory of Knowing*
See page: 27

Grelling, Kurt
Dates: 1886–1942
Nationality: German
See pages: 157

Helmhotz, Hermann von
Dates: 1821–1894
Nationality: German
Most famous work: *Über die Erhaltung der Kraft*
See page: 31

Heraclitus
Dates: 535–475 BCE
Nationality: Greek
See pages: 14, 21

Hilbert, David
Dates: 1862–1943
Nationality: German
See page: 164, 166–167

Hobbes, Thomas
Dates: 1588–1679
Nationality: British
Most famous work: *Leviathan*
See page: 29

Hume, David
Dates: 1711–1776
Nationality: Scottish
Most famous work:
Treatise of Human Nature
See pages: 29, 44–45, 87, 93, 99, 108, 141, 146, 161, 167

Huxley, T. H.
Dates: 1825–1895
Nationality: British
See page: 109

James, William
Dates: 1842–1910
Nationality: American
Most famous work:
Principles of Psychology
See pages: 109, 118–119

Jesus
Dates: 8/2 BCE–29/36 CE
Nationality: Judean
See pages: 54, 59, 66, 70

Johnson, Samuel
Dates: 1696–1772
Nationality: British
Most famous work:
Elementa Philosophica
See page: 33

Kant, Immanuel
Dates: 1724–1804
Nationality: German
Most famous work:
Critique of Pure Reason
See pages: 54–55, 66, 82, 97, 108, 113, 141, 146, 153

La Mettrie, Julien Offray de
Dates: 1709–1751
Nationality: French
See page: 108

Lao Tzu
Dates: 4th/6th Century BCE
Nationality: Chinese
Most famous work:
Tao Te Ching (Laozi)
See page: 18

Lehrer, Keith
Dates: b. 1936
Nationality: American
See page: 27

Leibniz, Gottfried Wilhelm
Dates: 1646–1716
Nationality: German
See pages: 29, 164

Locke, John
Dates: 1632–1704
Nationality: British
Most famous work:
Essay Concerning Human Understanding
See pages: 29, 32, 66, 101, 109

Martyr, Justin
Dates: 100–165
Nationality: Judean
See page: 15

Mencius
Dates: 372–289 BCE
Nationality: Chinese
Most famous work:
Mencius (also spelled *Mengzi* or *Meng-tzu*)
See page: 78

Michotte, Albert
Dates: 1881–1965
Nationality: Belgian
Most famous work:
The Perception of Causality
See page: 99

Mill, John Stuart
Dates: 1806–1873
Nationality: British
See page: 68

Newton, Sir Isaac
Dates: 1643–1727
Nationality: British
Most famous works:
Philosophiae Naturalis;
Principia Mathematica
See page: 164

Noddings, Nel
Dates: b. 1929
Nationality: American
See page: 70

Occam, William of
Dates: 1288–1348
Nationality: British
Most famous work:
Summa Logicae
See page: 92, 154

Pascal, Blaise
Dates: 1623–1662
Nationality: French
See page: 118

Paxson, Thomas
Dates: –
Nationality: American
See page: 27

Philo of Megara
Dates: 4th Century BCE
Nationality: Greek
Most famous work:
Menexenos
See page: 138

Plato
Dates: 428–348 BCE
Nationality: Greek
Most famous work:
The Republic
See pages: 13, 15, 19, 20–21, 26, 38, 45, 55, 57, 62, 63, 87, 90, 91, 92, 96, 104–105

Protagoras
Dates: 490–420 BCE
Nationality: Greek
Most famous work:
Antilogies
See pages: 14, 149

Pyrrho of Elis
Dates: 360–270 BCE
Nationality: Greek
See pages: 24–25

Pythagoras
Dates: 580–500 BCE
Nationality: Greek
Most famous work:
Pythagorean Theorem
See pages: 15, 88–89, 131

Quine, Willard Van Orman
Dates: 1908–2000
Nationality: American
Most famous work:
"Two Dogmas of Empiricism"
See page: 6

Rawls, John
Dates: 1921–2002
Nationality: American
Most famous work:
A Theory of Justice
See page: 66

Rousseau, Jean-Jacques
Dates: 1712–1778
Nationality: Swiss
Most famous work:
The Social Contract
See page: 66

Russell, Bertrand
Dates: 1872–1970
Nationality: British
Most famous work:
Principia Mathematica
See pages: 140, 146, 157, 164–165

Sankara
Dates: 788–820
Nationality: Indian
Most famous work:
Viveka Chudamani
See page: 86

Sartre, Jean-Paul
Dates: 1905–1980
Nationality: French
Most famous work:
Being and Nothingness
See page: 51

Singer, Peter
Dates: b. 1946
Nationality: Australian
See page: 68

Socrates
Dates: 470–399 BCE
Nationality: Greek
Most famous work:
Socratic Method
See pages: 6, 13, 14–15, 20–23, 38, 57, 62–63, 90–91

Spinoza, Baruch
Dates: 1632–1677
Nationality: Dutch
Most famous work: *Ethica Ordine Geometrico Demonstrata*
See pages: 87, 113

Thales of Miletus
Dates: 624–546 BCE
Nationality: Greek
See page: 14

Tseng Tzu
Dates: 505–436 BCE
Nationality: Chinese
See page: 79

Wason, P. C.
Dates: 1924–2003
Nationality: British
Most famous work:
Wason Selection Task
See pages: 16–17

Wittgenstein, Ludwig
Dates: 1889–1951
Nationality: Austrian
Most famous work:
Tractatus Logico–Philosophicus
See pages: 140–141

Xenophanes
Dates: 570–480 BCE
Nationality: Greek
See page: 24

Zeno of Elea
Dates: 490?–430 BCE?
Nationality: Greek
Most famous work:
Zeno's Paradoxes
See pages: 150–151, 164

INDEX

REFERENCES

Standard examples, puzzles, paradoxes, and lore are used throughout, often without reference. In many cases, to improve readability, in-line citations have been left out, so references appear here chapter by chapter, in order of use. (Sources used in more than one chapter are not repeated.) Classic or ancient sources given in the text are sometimes not repeated here, or commonly available editions in English are indicated.

Chapter I

Annas, J., and J. Barnes. *The Modes of Scepticism: Ancient Texts and Modern Interpretations*: Cambridge University Press, 1985.

Cornford, Francis M. *Before and After Socrates*: Cambridge University Press, 1932.

Taylor, A. E. *Socrates: the Man and his Thought*. New York: Doubleday Anchor, 1933.

Heine, S. J., and D. R. Lehman. "Culture, self-discrepancies, and self-satisfaction." *Personality and Social Psychology Bulletin*. 25, 915–925, 1999.

Hong, Y., M. W. Morris, C. Chiu, and V. Benet-Martinez. "Multicultural minds: A dynamic constructivist approach to culture and cognition." *American Psychologist*, 55, 709–720, 2000.

Jones, E. E., and V. A. Harris. "The attribution of attitudes." *Journal of Experimental Social Psychology* 3, 1–24, 1967.

Lindsay, D. S., D. L. Paulhus, and J. S. Nairne. *Psychology: The Adaptive Mind*. 3rd Ed. Thomson Nelson, 2007.

Miller, J. G. "Culture and the development of everyday social explanation." *Personality and Social Psychology Bulletin*. 20, 592–978. 1984.

Norenzayan, A., I. Choi, and R. E. Nisbett. "Cultural similarities and differences in social inference: Evidence from behavioral predictions and lay theories of behavior." *Personality and Social Psychology Bulletin*. 28, 109–120, 2002.

Ross, L. "The intuitive psychologist and his shortcomings: Distortions in the attribution process." *Advances in Experimental Social Psychology*. Edited by Berkowitz, L. 0, 173–220. New York: Academic Press, 1977.

Wason, P. C. "Reasoning about a rule." *Quarterly Journal of Experimental Psychology*, 20, 273–281, 1968.

Wason, P. C., and P. N. Johnson-Laird. "A conflict between selecting and evaluating information in an inferential task." *British Journal of Psychology*, 68, 325–31, 1970.

Cleary, Thomas. *The Essential Tao*. San Francisco: Harper, 1991.

Chuang Tzu. *Basic Writings*. Translated by Watson, Burton. New York: Columbia University Press, 1964.

Burtt, E. A., Ed. *The Teachings of the Compassionate Buddha*. New York: New American Library, 1955.

Radhakrishnan, S., and C. A. Moore, Eds. *A Source Book in Indian Philosophy*. Princeton University Press, 1957.

Plato. *The Collected Dialogues of Plato*. Edited by E. Hamilton and H. Cairns. Princeton University Press, 1980.

Smith, T. V., Ed. *From Thales to Plato*. University of Chicago Press, 1956.

Descartes, R. *The Philosophical Writings of Descartes*, Vols. 1–2. Translated by Cottingham, J., Stoothoff, R., and Murdoch, D. Cambridge University Press, 1985.

Gettier, Edmund L. "Is Justified True Belief Knowledge?" *Analysis*, 23, 121–23, 1963.

Goldman, Alvin. "A Causal Theory of Knowing." *The Journal of Philosophy*. 64, 335–372, 1967.

Lehrer, K., and T. Paxson. "Knowledge: Undefeated Justified True Belief." *The Journal of Philosophy*, 66, 1–22, 1969.

Locke, John. *An Essay Concerning Human Understanding*. 1689.

Moore, G. E. "Proof of an External World." *Proceedings of the British Academy*, 25, 273–300, 1939.

Chomsky, Noam. *Knowledge of Language: Its nature, origin and use*. New York: Praeger, 1986.

Hume, David. *A Treatise of Human Nature*. Edited by Selby-Bigge, L. A. 2nd ed. revised by Nidditch, P. H. Oxford: Clarendon Press, 1978. (Originally published 1739–40).

Chapter 2

Sartre, Jean-Paul. *Existentialism and Humanism.* Translated and introduced by Philip Mairet. London: Methuen, 1948.

Hardin, G. "Tragedy of the Commons." *Science*, 162. 1243–1248, 1968.

Hardin, G. "Lifeboat Ethics: the Case Against Helping the Poor," in *Psychology Today*, 1974.

Aristotle. *The Complete Works of Aristotle*, Vols. 1–2. Edited by Jonathan Barnes. Princeton University Press, 1984.

Kant, Immanuel. *Grounding for the Metaphysics of Morals.* Translated by James W. Ellington, 3rd ed. Indianapolis: Hackett, 1993. (Originally published 1785).

Mill, J. S. *Utilitarianism*, 2nd ed. London: Longmans, 1861.

Williams, B. *Morality: An Introduction to Ethics.* New York: Harper and Row, 1972.

Williams, B. "A Critique of Utilitarianism," in *Utilitarianism: For and Against.* Cambridge University Press, 1973.

Gilligan, C. *In a Different Voice: Psychological Theory and Women's Development.* Cambridge: Harvard University Press, 1982.

Noddings, Nel. *Caring, a Feminine Approach to Ethics and Moral Education.* Berkeley: University of California Press, 1984.

Wing-Tsit Chan. *A Sourcebook in Chinese Philosophy.* Princeton University Press, 1963.

Narada Maha Thera. *A Manual of Abhidhamma.* 4th rev. ed. Kuala Lumpur: Buddhist Missionary Society, 1979.

Chapter 3

Galileo. *Discoveries and Opinions of Galileo.* Translated by Stillman Drake. New York: Doubleday Anchor Books, 1957.

Kant, Immanuel. *Critique of Pure Reason.* Translated by Kemp Smith, Norman, 3rd ed.. New York: St. Martin's Press, 1965. (Originally published 1781–1787).

Kant, Immanuel. *Prolegomena to Any Future Metaphysics.* Translated by Beck, L. W. Indianapolis: Bobbs-Merrill, 1950. (Originally published 1783).

Hume, David. *Enquiry Concerning Human Understanding*, edited by Selby-Bigge, L. A. 3rd ed. revised by Nidditch, P. H.. Oxford: Clarendon Press, 1975. (Originally published 1749).

Michotte, Albert. *The Perception of Causality.* Translated from French by T. R. Miles and E. Miles. New York: Basic Books, 1963.

Wegner, Daniel M.. *The Illusion of Conscious Will.* Cambridge: The MIT Press, 2002.

Spalding, K. L., R. D. Bhardwaj, B. A. Buchholz, H. Druid, J. Frisen. "Retrospective Birth Dating of Cells in Humans." *Cell*, 122, (1), 133–143, 2005.

Wade, Nicolas. "Your Body Is Younger Than You Think." *New York Times Science.* http://www.nytimes.com, August 2, 2005.

Fechner, Gustav. *Elemente der Psychophysik.* 1861.

La Mettrie, Julian. *L'Homme Machine.* 1749.

Huxley, Thomas Henry. "On the Hypothesis that Animals Are Automata, and Its History." 1874.

James, William. "Does 'Consciousness' Exist?" *Journal of Philosophy, Psychology, and Scientific Methods*, 1, 477–491, 1904.

Spinoza, B. *The Ethics and Selected Letters.* Translated by Shirley, Samuel. Indianapolis: Hackett, 1682.

Mascaro, J., Trans. *The Upanishads.* London: Penguin Books, 1965.

James, William. *The Will to Believe.* New World, 1896.

Carrithers, M. *The Buddha.* Oxford University Press, 1983.

Dhammapada: The Path of Perfection. Translated by Mascaro, Juan. London: Penguin, 1973.

Chapter 4

Sextus Empiricus: Selections from the Major Writings on Scepticism, Man, and God. Edited by Philip P. Hallie. Indianapolis: Hackett, 1985.

Carrol, Lewis. *Symbolic Logic and The Game of Logic.* New York: Dover, 1958.

Wittgenstein, Ludwig. *Tractatus Logico-Philosophicus.* Translated by Ogden and Richards. London: Routledge and Kegan Paul, 1922.

Wittgenstein, Ludwig. *Philosophical Investigations.* 2nd ed. Translated by G. E. M. Anscombe. Oxford: Basil Blackwell, 1958.

Frege, Gottlob. *Begriffsschrift und andere Aufsatze,* translated as *Conceptual Notation, and Related Articles* by Bynum, T. W.. Oxford: Clarendon, 1972. (Originally published in 1879).

Frege, Gottlob. *Grundlagen der Arithmetik,* translated as *The Foundations of Arithmetic: a Logico-mathematical Enquiry into the Concept of Number* by J. L. Austin. Oxford: Blackwell, 1953. (Originally published in 1884).

Boolos, George. "To Be is to be a Value of a Variable (or to be Some Values of Some Variables)." *Journal of Philosophy.* 81: 430–49, 1984.

Wang, Hao. *Reflections on Kurt Gödel.* Cambridge: The MIT Press, 1987.

CREDITS

This book was almost not a book. It was written late and in a hurry. When I look it over now, I see my teachers. I hope they see themselves here too—if they still see—and are not displeased.

My debt to other scholars is clear to me on every page; the list of references at the end only partially records that debt, and it was much cut back to fit the popular tone and the limited space available. Besides packaging, there is little new here. I accept all responsibility for error.

Special thanks are due to Profs. Verena Huber-Dyson and Gary Miller, who each read parts of Chapter 4. And my warm appreciation goes to Mona L. Haywood, who read over much of the book and helped in ways too numerous to mention.

I have Ian Whitelaw to thank the most. He found me, asked my help, and instead helped me. He read everything and wrote or drafted several spreads (Gettier Problems; Problems of Self-Reference; the first four spreads of Chapter 2; This is not a Bike; Ultimate Choices; Fallacy Spotting; Induction); and he assisted greatly with

exercises and examples throughout. He was constantly encouraging and gently kept me on the ball. All this while angling whitewater, wrestling llamas, and braving fierce windstorms. I must get out more often.

I owe Nigel Browning at Quid Publishing the title, and indeed the whole idea for the book. James Evans has been a more enjoyable combination of patience and push than he suspects. I owe him a beer at the Last Chance Saloon.

Tony Seddon designed the book and provided the brilliant illustrations—I couldn't be happier with them. I know nameless others helped along the way. To them I name my thanks.

It is all more than I asked for. Yet my gratitude exceeds the gift. Thanks, all.

For George and Jean, who did not live to see it.